MW01061885

THE PARADOXES OF DELUSION

Wittgenstein, Schreber, and the Schizophrenic Mind

ALSO BY LOUIS A. SASS

MADNESS
AND
MODERNISM:
Insanity
in the
Light of
Modern Art,
Literature, and Thought

THE PARADOXES OF DELUSION

Wittgenstein, Schreber, and the Schizophrenic Mind

LOUIS A. SASS

CORNELL UNIVERSITY PRESS ITHACA AND LONDON

First published 1994 by Cornell University Press.

International Standard Book Number 0-8014-2210-8
Library of Congress Catalog Card Number 93-24931
Printed in the United States of America
Librarians: Library of Congress cataloging information appears on the last page of the book.

♾ The paper in this book meets the minimum requirements of the American National Standard for Information Sciences—Permanence of Paper for Printed Library Materials, ANSI Z39.48-1984.

TO

SHIRA

CONTENTS

PREFACE

You must always be puzzled by mental illness. The thing I would dread most, if I became mentally ill, would be your adopting a common sense attitude; that you could take it for granted that I was deluded.

—Ludwig Wittgenstein, quoted in *Recollections of Wittgenstein*

This is an essay on philosophy and madness—on madness as akin to philosophy, on philosophy as a kind of madness. There are two principal characters: Daniel Paul Schreber, a jurist in the kingdom of Saxony who became insane in midlife and spent thirteen years in mental asylums between 1884 and his death in 1911; and Ludwig Wittgenstein, the philosopher from Vienna and then Cambridge who has been such a central figure in the development of twentieth-century thought. This may seem an odd or even outlandish pairing, but it is by no means an arbitrary one.

Schreber has been described as the most famous madman in the history of psychiatry. He is the author of *Memoirs of My Nervous Illness*, an intricately detailed, lucid, yet bizarre volume that was read by Sigmund Freud, Eugen Bleuler, Karl Jaspers, and other psychiatric writers of the early twentieth century and used by them as a key example of paranoia and especially of schizophrenia. Through his autobiographical book, Schreber's example has exerted a singularly powerful influence on images and conceptualizations of insanity in modern psychiatry; to consider his account is to investigate what is perhaps the paradigm case of madness in our time.

Wittgenstein (1889–1951) is widely acknowledged as the greatest philosopher of the twentieth century but—more important for our purposes—he was also a kind of antiphilosopher, the most acute diagnostician and profound critic of the illusions and contradictions to which the philosophical mind is prone. "The philosopher," he wrote, "is the man who has to cure himself of many sicknesses of the understanding before he can arrive at the notions of sound human understanding"; in Wittgenstein's view such a cure could only be attained through a changed mode not just of thought but of living (RFM, 157, 57). As we shall see, Wittgenstein's characterization can almost be taken literally: the sicknesses of the understanding he examined in his later work, sicknesses bound up with the philosopher's predilection for abstraction and alienation—for detachment from body, world, and community—have a great deal in common with the symptoms displayed by Schreber and many other mental patients with schizophrenic or related forms of illness. Wittgenstein's critical reflections on philosophy can, in fact, provide us with insight into some of the key enigmas of insanity, and in particular into the nature of delusions, which are perhaps the most important and widely known of all psychiatric symptoms yet, at the same time, among the least understood.

A great weakness of twentieth-century psychiatry and clinical psychology, at least in the United States, has been a tendency to neglect careful description and analysis of abnormal psychological phenomena in favor of a too-quick and too-exclusive focus on etiology or causation. In practice this has meant that the nuances and complexities of psychopathological signs and symptoms tend to be ignored; too often we rely on the complacency and presumption of a misleading kind of "common sense," an attitude that dismisses peculiar forms of action and experience as but inferior versions of the norm. Thus delusions, generally considered the hallmark of insanity, are taken to be little more than instances of error—mistaken beliefs in a mind lacking the powers of reason. But as the more discerning experts have long recognized, delusions, at least in schizophrenia, are far more complicated than this traditional conceptualization implies. The more closely one examines them, in fact, the stranger they may appear, and the more they seem to elude definition.

Wittgenstein's reflections have the advantage of allowing us to recover the sense of puzzlement, even wonder, that such phenomena ought to arouse—and then to move beyond this to another level of understanding, one that can help us make some sense of the delusional world without slighting its subtleties or its paradoxes.

I had the initial idea for this book some years ago, but I originally conceived it as only a part, perhaps a chapter, of a larger project I was then beginning (recently published as *Madness and Modernism: Insanity in the Light of Modern Art, Literature, and Thought*). As I delved further into Wittgenstein and into Schreber, however, connections began to proliferate at a surprising rate. More and more elements of Wittgenstein's thought came to seem relevant, more aspects of Schreber's experience began to make sense; further, the very existence of these affinities, with their suggestion of similar existential preoccupations, seemed to cast new light on underlying motivations that might lend unity and coherence to Wittgenstein's diverse preoccupations as a philosopher (the latter is an issue I hope to pursue more deeply in a later publication). Given the canonical status of the Schreber memoir and the psychiatric significance of the problem of delusion, along with Wittgenstein's central importance as an exemplar and critic of modern thought, a more extensive treatment seemed warranted; so eventually I gave in and allowed these reflections to turn into a book.

These ideas germinated during a very enjoyable and productive year I spent as a member of the Institute for Advanced Study (School of Social Science), where I was supported by a fellowship from the National Endowment for the Humanities. I am very grateful to the Institute as well as to the Endowment for encouraging and supporting my early exploration of these themes. More recently, I was the beneficiary of a Henry Rutgers Research Fellowship awarded by Rutgers University.

Several people made useful comments on earlier versions or parts of this work, including George Atwood, Patricia Dacey, Sander Gilman, Lars Hem, Charles Palliser, Sybe Terwee, Fred Wertz, and several students of theoretical psychology from the University of Leiden; my thanks to all of them. Thanks also to Michèle Nayman. A careful, incisive, yet sympathetic reading by Karen Hanson was especially helpful, as were the many insightful comments so generously offered by my friend James Walkup. I am also indebted to John

Ackerman of Cornell University Press for encouragement, patience, and general kindness as well as for some discerning editorial suggestions that improved the final version.

My deepest appreciation goes to two people. To Shira Nayman—for helping me to think through my arguments, for editorial comments that served to clarify and enliven the text, and, most of all, for spurring me more than once past the slough of despond. And to my father (formerly a student of philosophy)—who taught me to question the question and, more generally, inspired what I sometimes think of as a Wittgensteinian frame of mind (though he would never call it that).

LOUIS A. SASS

New York City

ABBREVIATIONS

Works by Schreber and Wittgenstein are cited in parentheses in the text.

Schreber: M = Daniel Paul Schreber, *Memoirs of My Nervous Illness*, trans. Ida Macalpine and Richard Hunter (Cambridge: Harvard University Press, 1988; previously published in English by Wm. Dawson, London, 1955; first published in German in 1903). In addition to the memoir, this book includes a psychiatric introduction and legal documentation from Schreber's commitment proceedings. Reference is to the page numbering of the English edition. M, orig = the German edition: Schreber, *Denkwürdigkeiten eines Nervenkranken* (Frankfurt: Ullstein, 1973). Reference to page numbers in the German edition is to the original pagination, given in brackets in the 1973 reprint.

Wittgenstein: BBB = *The Blue and Brown Books* (Oxford: Basil Blackwell, 1958). CV = *Culture and Value*, trans. Peter Winch, ed. G. H. von Wright (Chicago: University of Chicago Press, 1980). L = "Wittgenstein's Lectures in 1930–33," notes recorded and paraphrased by G. E. Moore, *Mind* 64 (1955), 1–27. NB = *Notebooks 1914–1916*, 2d ed., trans. G. E. M. Anscombe, ed. G. H. von Wright and G. E. M. Anscombe (Chicago: University of Chicago Press, 1979). NFL = "Wittgenstein's Notes for Lectures on 'Private Experience' and 'Sense Data'," ed. Rush Rhees, *Philosophical Review* 77 (1968), 271–320. OC = *On Certainty*, trans. G. E. M. Anscombe and G. H. von Wright (New York: Harper and Row, 1969). PI = *Philosophical Investigations*, trans. G. E. M. Anscombe (Oxford: Basil Blackwell, 1953). With the *Philosophical Investigations*, I follow the convention of citing paragraph numbers for Part I (always preceded by §) and page numbers for Part II. RFM = *Remarks on the Foundations of Mathematics*, trans. G. E. M. Anscombe, ed. G. H. von Wright, Rush Rhees, and G. E. M. Anscombe (Oxford: Basil Blackwell, 1956). RPPII = *Remarks on the Philosophy of Psychology*, Vol. 2 (Oxford: Oxford University Press, 1980). TLP = *Tractatus Logico-Philosophicus*, trans. D. F. Pears and B. F. McGuinness (London: Routledge and Kegan Paul, 1961). This work is cited by section number. Z = *Zettel*, trans. G. E. M. Anscombe, ed. G. E. M. Anscombe and G. H. von Wright (Berkeley: University of California Press, 1970).

THE PARADOXES OF DELUSION

Wittgenstein, Schreber, and the Schizophrenic Mind

If in life we are surrounded by death, so too in the health of our intellect we are surrounded by madness."

—Ludwig Wittgenstein, *Culture and Value*

Theoretical egoism [solipsism] can never be demonstrably refuted, yet in philosophy it has never been used otherwise than as a sceptical sophism, i.e., a pretence. As a serious conviction, on the other hand, it could only be found in a madhouse, and as such it stands in need of a cure rather than a refutation."

—Arthur Schopenhauer, *The World as Will and Idea*

INTRODUCTION

Insanity has generally been assumed to be a matter of perceiving things that do not exist and believing things that are not true. As Karl Jaspers (an influential psychiatrist before he became a philosopher) put it, "Since time immemorial, delusion has been taken as the basic characteristic of madness. To be mad was to be deluded."[1] Such a view certainly prevails in contemporary psychiatry, clinical psychology, and psychoanalysis, where disturbance in or failure of "reality-testing" is considered to be the defining criterion for diagnosing a so-called psychotic condition.[2] Considering its pivotal role in psychiatric diagnosis and theory, this quintessential sign of madness—generally known as "poor reality-testing"—has received surprisingly little critical attention. In my view, this fundamental principle of psychiatry is either hopelessly misleading or just plain wrong, at least when applied to many patients with the most severe and paradigmatic kind of insanity: schizophrenia.

A classic statement of the traditional view was offered by the psychoanalyst Paul Federn in 1949:

> The basis of sanity is correct and automatic recognition of [the] breach between subjective mental individual experiences in the world and the

> knowledge of the status of the world as it actually exists. Sanity means dealing with the world and with oneself with the faculty of distinguishing clearly between them. It is therefore obvious that in schizophrenia it is the ego that is ill.[3]

According to the standard interpretation, psychotics are those who fail to distinguish adequately between the real and the imaginary in that they treat the imaginary realm as if it *were* real. In the movie *I Never Promised You a Rose Garden*, for instance, the supposedly schizophrenic protagonist repeatedly turns round to see Neanderthal men and women squatting in the hospital ward. Despite their actual nonexistence, to the fictional patient of the movie these hallucinated Neanderthals seem as real, and as frightening, as can be.

Such a conception of the inner world of insanity is as widely accepted in psychiatry and psychology as among the general public. One supposes that, whereas there is disturbance in the content of patients' worlds (*what* they believe and perceive is unrealistic or illogical), the form of those worlds (the overall "structure" or "feel," the *way* they believe what they believe) is essentially normal. That is, such patients are assumed to believe in the content of their delusions—or at least to want to believe in this content—with the same sense of objective reality that normal people ascribe to the facts of their actual and consensual worlds. "What objectively are delusions and hallucinations are to him unassailable truth and adequate motive for action" (M, 282), wrote the superintendent of Sonnenstein asylum in 1900 in a legal brief arguing for the involuntary incarceration of Daniel Paul Schreber, the paranoid schizophrenic whose bizarre experiences are the focus of this book.

The origins of this now orthodox conception of insanity can be traced to the mid-seventeenth century, a time when the rationalism of the Enlightenment was beginning to replace the religious worldview of the Renaissance. During the Renaissance, the figure of the madman (or that of the fool, for the two were inseparable) had roused profound ambivalence: the madman was an object of ridicule but also of fascination and respect. Though he was, on the one hand, an innocent or an instrument of vice, he was also imagined as having access to a truth more profound than that available to normal people. Indeed, the very existence of the wise fool suggested its reverse: the folly of "wisdom" and of all who are conventionally wise; thus the madman was able to offer satiric insight into the folly of human society and tragic insight into human nature, as in Erasmus's *In Praise of Folly* or in *King Lear*, where madness gives Lear the wisdom he lacked as a king.[4] Michel Foucault has argued that, with the dawning of Enlightenment rationalism, the possibility of this alternative vision, this critical perspective on conventional reason, was erased. In the "Classical Age," as Foucault calls the age of reason, insanity came to be viewed as mere unreason, a simple condition of mistakenness, of failure to reason and perceive accurately. Madness was silenced, its claim to wisdom dismissed, when it came to be viewed as a quasi-sleep that lacks "the consciousness of deluded consciousness," the awareness of the illusory nature of its illusions.[5] The contemporary poor reality-testing formula is the perpetuation of this view which considers madness and insight to be as antithetical as error and truth.[6]

Schizophrenia is the most severe form of psychosis and the one whose history is nearly identical with that of psychiatry itself; it has, with good reason, been called the "sacred symbol of psychiatry" and the "madness *par excellence*" of our time.[7] Yet there are many such patients whose delusions hardly seem to jibe with the poor reality-testing formula. As the psychiatrist Eugen Bleuler observed during his long career at the Burghölzli hospital in Switzerland, most schizophrenic patients certainly do not *act* as if they mistook their delusions for reality: "Kings and Emperors, Popes and Redeemers engage, for the most part, in quite banal work, provided they have any energy at all for activity. This is true not only of patients in institutions, but also of those who are completely free. None of our generals has ever attempted to act in accordance with his imaginary rank and station."[8]

Many schizophrenic patients seem to experience their delusions and hallucinations as having a special quality or feel that sets these apart from their "real" beliefs and perceptions, or from reality as experienced by the "normal" person. Indeed, such patients often seem to have a surprising, and rather disconcerting, kind of insight into their own condition. Bleuler describes one patient with hebephrenic schizophrenia who would make fun of himself because he, the Lord and "King of the Whole World," had been accustomed to making the weather immediately after teatime yet did not know how to get out of the hospital. The patient asked himself "whether all this did not sound rather fantastic."[9] At times, in fact, one may even begin to suspect, in the presence of such patients, that they are somehow only playacting—as if, like the protagonist of Pirandello's *Henry IV*, they are just feigning madness while taking a perverse delight in forcing those around them to support the charade.

The standard definitions—delusion as "incorrect belief," hallucination as "perception without an object"—hardly seem helpful in characterizing such schizophrenics. If taken literally, such definitions are often wrong; taken more loosely, they simply indicate a mystery that requires further investigation and analysis. But how *can* we understand this perplexing kind of existence? Is it even possible for a nonschizophrenic person to empathize with or comprehend this alien form of life?

One expert who did not believe in the possibility of either an empathic or an intellectual comprehension of such patients is Jaspers, certainly one of the most subtle observers in the history of modern psychiatry. In his monumental *General Psychopathology*, Jaspers described schizophrenic patients' attitudes toward their delusions as involving a "specific schizophrenic incorrigibility" that is quite unlike the normal dogmatism of fanatical people or of other types of psychotics such as manic-depressives. In "delusion proper," as Jaspers called the specifically schizophrenic symptom, belief is absolutely unshakable, quite beyond argument. "Well, that is how it is," the patient will say. "I have no doubts about it. I know it is so." And yet, by a seeming paradox, the patient's attitude toward his delusions is, in Jaspers's words, "peculiarly inconsequent at times." "Reality for him does not always carry the same meaning as that of normal reality."[10] Despite the certainty with which they are held, such delusions typically do not lead to action, at least not to the kind of action that would seem reasonable given what the patient seems to be claiming.

Schizophrenics' delusions differ in this respect from the "overvalued ideas" of many patients with severe (but nonpsychotic) personality disorders, for example, paranoid personalities. Though such overvalued ideas are not as firmly held as schizophrenic delusions, they are far more likely to be acted on, often in a determined and persistent way.[11] And, in contrast with the delusions of most patients with affective psychoses, such as manic-depressive illness, the delusions of schizophrenics are not accompanied by emotional states appropriate to their contents. In these ways, among others, the schizophrenic delusional experience contradicts the usual notion of poor reality testing, with its implication that an objectively *inaccurate* perception or belief is taken by the patient as real. What seems distinctive about such "delusional" worlds—and what needs to be explained—is in fact the strange tendency of such patients to accord great importance to their delusions while nevertheless seeming to experience these same delusions as being, in some sense, irrelevant or unreal.

A second feature Jaspers considered to be characteristic of schizophrenia is what he called the "delusional atmosphere" or "mood"—an overwhelming but almost indescribable transformation of the perceptual world that often precedes or accompanies the development of delusions. In this peculiar state of mind (to be discussed in detail in Chapter 3) the perceptual world seems to have undergone some subtle but all-encompassing change: unfamiliar events and objects may seem like copies or repetitions of themselves; perceptual phenomena may seem tremendously specific and deeply meaningful, but without the patient being able to explain why.[12] This characteristic mood state, which is exceedingly hard to put into words, seems to be visually evoked by the paintings of the protosurrealist Giorgio de Chirico—those shadowless cityscapes of infinite precision and uncanny meaningfulness with names like "The Enigma of the Day" and "The Mystery and Melancholy of a Street."[13]

Jaspers considered such qualities as the "specific schizophrenic incorrigibility" and the "delusional mood" to be crucial criteria for delusion proper; in fact, he even stated that a belief that was objectively true could nevertheless be considered a delusion if these qualities were present. And, he insisted, the qualities at issue could not be explained as resulting from a weakening of intelligence or logic or from mere confusion or clouding of consciousness. As he pointed out, delusions can and often do occur without any formal disturbances of thinking or any loss of the critical faculty.[14] Further, he argued that these symptoms ought to be sharply distinguished from the atmosphere of "delusion-like ideas" found in manic and depressive psychoses, for only the latter seemed to develop in an understandable way out of the intensity of previous experiences or emotional states. Indeed, Jaspers believed that these and other specific qualities of the delusional world of schizophrenia rendered such patients completely alien—so mysterious that they must always remain essentially incomprehensible, beyond empathy or the possibility of psychological explanation. With his central "axiom of the abyss," Jaspers even claimed that an interviewer's very feeling of encountering in the patient an absolutely enigmatic mode of life was the best way of diagnosing schizophrenia—a condition that supposedly involves some total alteration of the whole personality and lived-world, probably on a physiological basis, "the nature of which we are so far unable to describe, let alone formulate into a concept."[15] Much of contemporary "medical-model" psychiatry follows the spirit, if not the letter, of Jasper's approach: treating schizophrenia as a mere epiphenomenon of some biological dysfunction or deficiency and downplaying the possibility and importance of seeking a psychological interpretation, or an understanding from within, of the experiential world of the schizophrenic individual.

In this book I attempt to do what, according to Jaspers, cannot be done: to comprehend both empathically and conceptually some of the most bizarre and mysterious symptoms of schizophrenia. Though I illustrate my argument with examples from many different patients, my focus is on a single paranoid schizophrenic, the famous Daniel Paul Schreber. If schizophrenia is the prototypical form of madness, Schreber is the prototypical madman. His special significance derives from his autobiographical book, *Memoirs of My Nervous Illness* (*Denkwürdigkeiten eines Nervenkranken* in the original German).[16]

Schreber's memoirs, which Elias Canetti calls "the most important document in psychiatric literature," made their author perhaps the most famous and influential patient in the history of psychiatry.[17] Though the book, which contains virtually all the classic symptoms of both schizophrenia and paranoia, is seldom read, it has played a major role in forming modern conceptions of schizophrenia, of paranoia, and of psychosis in general. The *Memoirs* had a decisive impact on psychoanalytic conceptions, since it provided the material for the only case study Freud ever wrote of a psychotic patient, his famous "Psychoanalytic Notes Upon an Autobiographical Account of a Case of Paranoia (Dementia Paranoides)" of 1911.[18] Further, the psychiatrists who developed our modern notions of schizophrenia and dementia praecox (the older term for schizophrenia; dementia paranoides is the equivalent of paranoid schizophrenia)—including Eugen Bleuler, Karl Jaspers, and Carl Jung—also studied Schreber's account, extracting from it crucial examples of classic schizophrenic symptoms for inclusion in their *Ur*-texts of descriptive psychiatry.[19] And Schreber continues to be cited as a paradigmatic case of the schizophrenic diagnosis in contemporary psychiatry.[20]

Schreber was a highly intelligent and articulate man who rose to the position of appeals court judge in Dresden in 1893. He suffered several paranoid schizophrenic breakdowns in which he manifested virtually the whole panoply of classic psychotic signs and symptoms in all their bizarreness, "inappropriateness," and apparent primitivity. Sometimes, for example, he would be incontinent, and it was not unusual for him to break out into a loud and incomprehensible bellowing or laughter, to wear cheap jewelry or other feminine adornment, or to stand in rigid immobility for hours on end, muttering phrases and grimacing into the sun (M, 4). At times he would make cryptic assertions, insisting, for instance, that there had been a "loss of rays" or that the doctor was "negligently emitting rays" (M, 268). But Schreber's most prominent symptoms involved the elaborate delusions—"so-called delusions," he called them—that are elaborated in his *Memoirs*. There he claims, for example, that he was being transformed into a woman, and he describes a veritable private cosmos of "nerves," "rays," "souls," and "gods" who are in constant interaction with one another or with himself. These "supernatural matters" are, he writes, "the most difficult subject ever to exercise the human mind": "I cannot of course count upon being *fully* understood because things are dealt with which cannot be expressed in human language." These matters which "exceed human understanding"—both Schreber's and that of his readers—can be expressed, he says, only in "images and similes," yet they are of incomparable importance: Schreber claims that he has been afforded "deeper insight than all other human beings" and that his book "belong[s] to the most interesting ones ever written since the existence of the world" (M, 301, 41, 184, 153, 289).

In what follows I argue that, despite the great importance he attributes to them, Schreber does not generally experience his delusions as being literally true but, rather, as having a certain "subjectivized" quality—that is, as being in some sense the product of his own consciousness rather than as enjoying an independent or objective existence (as the poor reality-testing formula implies). His mode of experience is in fact strikingly reminiscent of the philosophical doctrine of solipsism, according to which the whole of reality, including the external world and other persons, is but a representation appearing to a single, individual self, namely, the self of the philosopher who holds the doctrine (claiming, for example, that only his or her own feelings and perceptions are real). Many of the details, complexities, and contradictions of Schreber's delusional world that seem inconsistent with the poor reality-testing formula can be understood in the light of solipsism, at least if we accept and carefully follow the analysis of this philosophical position offered in the later writings of Ludwig Wittgenstein. Solipsism was a recurrent, perhaps even an obsessional concern of Wittgenstein's philosophizing—or, perhaps more accurately put, of his antiphilosophizing (for Wittgenstein, like several other modern philosophers, was inclined to view himself as repudiating the very tradition of philosophy itself);[21] and his speculations on this topic, gnomic and difficult as they may at first appear, can provide a way of comprehending the inner logic of the strange worlds of many schizophrenics.

Wittgenstein is famous for likening much of traditional philosophy, with its irrepressible urge toward metaphysical speculation, to a kind of disease—even to a mental illness in need of therapy. His attitude toward philosophy is often reminiscent of that of Stultitia, the heroine of Erasmus's *In Praise of Folly* who ridicules the pedantic sophistry and speculative metaphysics of what she calls the "foolosophers."[22] In Erasmus's book, however, Stultitia is herself mad—a wise fool who shows up the foolishness of the wise—whereas Wittgenstein attributes madness and delusion to the person of the traditional philosopher whom he is, in a sense, trying to cure.

Solipsism was one of Wittgenstein's most central examples of a metaphysical or philosophical disease, a disease born not of ignorance or carelessness but of abstraction, self-consciousness, and disengagement from practical and social activity. He saw it as closely related to—at times as a kind of ultimate logical conclusion of—other philosophical diseases such as idealism or sense data phenomenalism (these are, briefly, the philosophical position that denies objective material entities and reduces existence to thought and the position that considers sensory experiences to be the grounding of all reality). The solipsist was the first subject of Wittgenstein's famous image of the fly in the fly-bottle—the philosopher whose own desperate convolutions, and blindness to common sense, keep him both restless and entrapped: "The solipsist flutters and flutters in the flyglass, strikes against the walls, flutters further. How can he be brought to rest?" (NFL, 300).[23] It was Wittgenstein's deeply felt intuition that the source of such diseases may lie not so much in false or meaningless doctrines per se as in the underlying attitude or existential stance that motivates or justifies them.

Wittgenstein's likening of traditional, metaphysical philosophy to madness is more than just a striking metaphor: many of the pathological tendencies of mind, the diseases of intellect, which he diagnoses in his favorite examples of philosophical illusion turn out to correspond with uncanny precision to the experiences of such insane patients as Schreber. Like the solipsist and other metaphysicians discussed by Wittgenstein, Schreber was convinced of both the profundity and the ineffability of his own special vision of reality—which derived, he believed, from some special insight not vouchsafed to the common man. And, like the metaphysics Wittgenstein criticizes, Schreber's metaphysical vision can be shown to be less a revelation of some higher reality than a projection of his own overly convoluted and disengaged stance toward existence. Accordingly, my main purpose here is an eminently Wittgensteinian one: to unravel, with as much care and simplicity as the subject allows, the self-deluding involutions of the schizophrenic "form of life"[24]—and thus to dissipate the atmosphere of unutterable mystery and profundity that surrounds such patients, often confusing them as much as those who seek to know them. Incidentally, though I continue to use the term "delusions" to refer to the symptoms under discussion, this should not be construed as indicating acceptance of the standard ways of understanding or defining these symptoms. I must also underscore the phenomenological or hermeneutic nature of my task: the goal is to understand rather than to explain, and I am not concerned here with the important, but quite different, questions of the possible neurobiological underpinnings, etiological origins, or developmental precursors of this condition.[25]

To some psychologists, it may seem odd to turn to philosophy for an analysis of the felt actualities of a lived-world, especially to a philosophy as subtle and complicated as Wittgenstein's. And yet the schizophrenic lived-world defies description in normal terms, as Jaspers's doctrine of incomprehensibility indicates and as many schizophrenics, Schreber included, seem to realize. Philosophical abstractions may, oddly enough, be the most apt way of capturing the actual feel of such a world, a point that the following words of one schizoaffective patient might suggest: "In order to explain the feeling of not being real, it is necessary to go into a long unreal definition of the feeling, for it is so far from reality that, in order to be made into a concrete real definition, it has to be described in an abstract, unreal way, if it is to be fully understood."[26]

Though Wittgenstein spoke more than once of the parallels between philosophy and madness, these have seldom been taken very seriously and, to my knowledge, have never been applied to the clinical subtleties of psychotic experience.[27] This failure is not, I think, merely the result of the disciplinary boundaries dividing philosophy from psychiatry and psychology; it is also due, in part, to the biasing effect of the metaphors and conceptual polarities underlying our notions of insanity. The standard conceptions, whether psychoanalytic or psychiatric, have nearly always presupposed the West's enduring equation of sanity with reason, insanity with passion and error—as if madness were necessarily a kind of stupidity or dementia or, in the terms of Plato's famous metaphor, a case of the wild horse of instinct overwhelming the charioteer's conscious control. How, given such images, could madness possibly have anything to do with philosophy, the purest exercise of rationality?

Actually, to assert—as I do—that the lived-world of schizophrenic delusion is characterized by what might be called subjectivization may at first sound fairly consistent with these classic images. The traditional assumption, however, is that schizophrenic patients project subjective meanings onto the objective world, not that they have at least an implicit awareness of these meanings *as* subjective. Further, those who have attempted to understand or interpret schizophrenic delusions have nearly always understood the subjectivization in accordance with the psychoanalytic regression hypothesis, that is, as being a manifestation of a certain primitivization of consciousness: of regression to the id-dominated grandiosity and wish-fulfillment fantasizing of early infancy, or to immature forms of experience that precede development of a sense of self, of a capacity for self-critical metaawareness (consciousness of consciousness), or of the differentiation between subjective and objective, inner and outer.[28] And the position of radical antipsychiatric writers—Norman O. Brown, Gilles Deleuze and Félix Guattari, and R. D. Laing, for example—is surprisingly similar to the psychoanalytic one. They too see psychosis as something childlike or Dionysian, though they then make the romantic move of valorizing rather than pathologizing these supposedly primitive and uncontrolled conditions.[29]

In *Madness and Civilization*, Foucault describes the equation of pathology with primitivity as the product of a third period that follows the Renaissance and the Enlightenment, a "Modern Age" in which madness is domesticated and familiarized through being equated with childhood. Although Foucault often writes as if such modes of understanding were quite autonomous and discontinuous, even mutually incompatible, these ways of conceiving madness are often grafted onto one another in contemporary thought. Thus, though current medical-model psychiatry does express in rather pure form the Enlightenment view—madness as a state of deficiency, a condition of error—psychoanalysis manifests the legacies of both the Enlightenment and the Modern Age. In current psychoanalytic theory, the boundary between sanity and insanity continues to be demarcated by the sign of poor reality-testing, yet this sign is itself understood to be a manifestation of the infantile "ego functioning" or "ego boundaries" of the patient. In antipsychiatry, by contrast, we find something akin to the Renaissance respect for the wisdom and spontaneity of madness, qualities viewed as desirable consequences of regression to a childlike condition; in this sense, antipsychiatry combines the legacy of the Renaissance with that of the Modern Age.

We see, then, that schizophrenic delusions have been approached in a variety of ways: sometimes they are viewed as utterly incomprehensible; other times they are characterized all too simply—either as mistaken perceptions of a relatively normal lived-world or as equivalents of normal experiences of infancy. Wittgenstein's analysis of solipsism suggests a very different reading. Not only do I dispute the notion that schizophrenic delusions manifest 'poor reality-testing,' I also argue that the mode of consciousness in which these delusions are typically embedded is not, in its essence, truly primitive. In my view, the experience of many schizophrenic patients involves not an overwhelming by but a detachment from normal forms of emotion and desire,[30] not a loss but an exacerbation of various forms of self-conscious awareness; in many cases, schizophrenic lived-worlds seem to be dominated by motivations and concerns that are less libidinal than cognitive or epistemological in nature. Such an interpretation is far more consistent with the phenomenological peculiarities experienced by Schreber and many similar patients. Further, it can account for precisely those aspects of schizophrenia that have seemed to place these patients beyond the pale of any empathic comprehension.

The view I propose differs equally from the psychoanalytic, medical-model, and antipsychiatric positions—as it also does from the three legacies analyzed by Foucault, those of the Modern Age, the Enlightenment, and the Renaissance. Madness, on my reading, is neither the psyche's return to its primordial condition, nor the malfunctioning of reason, nor even some inspired alternative to human reason. It is, to be sure, a self-deceiving condition, but one that is generated from within rationality itself rather than by the loss of rationality. The parallels between Wittgenstein and Schreber reveal not a primitive or Dionysian condition but something akin to Wittgenstein's notion of a disease of the intellect, born at the highest pitches of self-consciousness and alienation. Madness, in this view, is the endpoint of the trajectory consciousness follows when it separates from the body and the passions, and from the social and practical world, and turns in upon itself; it is what might be called the mind's perverse self-apotheosis.

My juxtaposition of Wittgenstein and Schreber also has a second, and less explicit, purpose: to clarify Wittgenstein's speculations about solipsism (and certain related issues) by grounding these in the phenomenological reality of an actual lived-world. Wittgenstein is notoriously difficult to grasp. If those who seek to understand him have often had a hard time getting what his colleague John Wisdom called "a steady light giving an ordered view of what they wished to see,"[31] this may result less from the inherent obscurity of Wittgenstein's thought than from the difficulty in recognizing the existential relevance of the seemingly abstract problems with which he wrestles. A comparison of these two intractable domains—the thought of Wittgenstein and the phenomenology of a schizophrenic world—may allow each to illuminate the other.

Wittgenstein has sometimes been criticized for presenting philosophical objections to positions no philosopher has actually taken. Whether this is true is debatable; such an impression may derive, in any case, from the fact that Wittgenstein is often less concerned with specific doctrines than with certain tendencies of the mind, tendencies he recognizes both in himself and in others. Consequently his thoughts do not move in a conventionally ordered way from premise to conclusion, or even from critique of premise to critique of conclusion. His concerns are often more existential than logical—pertaining less to the content than the phenomenology or lived context of philosophical belief.

The difficulty of understanding Wittgenstein was perhaps captured best by Wittgenstein himself in a remark recalled by his sister Hermine. Hermine describes Ludwig's reaction when she expressed her inability to comprehend why he, with his incomparable philosophical mind, would rather work as a gardener's assistant or an elementary school teacher than as a professor of philosophy: "Ludwig replied with an analogy that reduced me to silence. He said, 'You remind me of somebody who is looking out through a closed window and cannot explain to himself the strange movements of a passer-by. He cannot tell what sort of storm is raging out there or that this person might only be managing with difficulty to stay on his feet.' Then I understood the state of mind he was in."[32]

Wittgenstein once wrote that, to a continuation of his philosophical work by others, he would prefer a change in the way people live, a change that would render superfluous all the issues and questions of his philosophizing (CV, 61). Such statements suggest that Wittgenstein's target is not just the logic but also the existential sources and conditions of philosophical illusion; indeed, he often seems less interested in refuting explicit philosophical doctrines than in diagnosing the whole attitude that tends to accompany not only these doctrines but the philosophizing stance or attitude in general. This stance, with its fostering of detached contemplation, abstraction, and introspection, is something with which Wittgenstein himself was, no doubt, all too familiar. Understanding the stance better, and in a more concrete way, may help us to comprehend something of the storm that accounts for the strange movements of Wittgenstein's antiphilosophizing—with its continual invocation, and its continual warding off, of the seductions of philosophy. It may also help to explain what Stanley Cavell has called the confessional nature of Wittgenstein's style of philosophical writing—with its deeply practical and negative nature, its concern with sensibility and inner change rather than with reasoning or dogma. For "in confessing," as Cavell pointed out, "you do not explain or justify, but describe how it is with you."[33]

The argument of Chapter 1 is fairly straightforward. I begin by elaborating in more detail certain points only sketched in this introduction; then I show how Wittgenstein's analysis of solipsism can account for aspects of the delusional world of Schreber and other schizophrenic patients which are inconsistent with standard notions of poor reality-testing. The picture becomes more complicated in Chapter 2, where I take up two features of the schizophrenic world which seem to contradict a solipsistic reading: the tendency of some schizophrenic patients to waver between a subjectivist stance and one that is more public and objective, and the tendency to lose a sense of the self's experiential centrality. Wittgenstein's analysis demonstrates how these seemingly antisolipsistic features may actually derive from solipsism's own paradoxical nature. In the third chapter I go beyond solipsism proper to treat two pervasive features of what might be called the atmosphere of the schizophrenic form of life: "phantom concreteness" and "mute particularity." Phantom concreteness is a difficult-to-describe quality of the experiential world in which phenomena that might be expected to be purely abstract, mental, or inner take on a certain substantialized and externalized quality. Mute particularity, in which the perceptual world takes on a quality of peculiar specificity, is the aforementioned aspect Jaspers considered to be the basis of what he called the delusional mood. Finally, in a conclusion, I compare my Wittgensteinian reading with other interpretations of Schreber—those by Freud, Elias Canetti, the psychoanalyst William Niederland, and the psychiatrist Morton Schatzman. By tracing a paradoxical logic in schizophrenic experience, my solipsistic interpretation reveals a surprising but powerful coherence underlying the complexities and apparent contradictions of Schreber's lived-world and that of many similar individuals.

Before proceeding, I should offer a few important caveats and qualifications. First, in discussing similarities between madness and certain kinds of philosophy I am not trying to equate the two or to deny all differences. For one thing, madness is an entire way of life, whereas philosophical views are predominantly intellectual positions that play a more restricted role in one's existence (though Wittgenstein does tend to erode this view of philosophy).

Let me also point out that my Wittgensteinian interpretation is not intended to apply to all phenomena termed "schizophrenic" in the psychiatric and psychoanalytic literature. Schizophrenia, after all, is a heterogeneous and contested concept—one that has been used to cover a variety of different subtypes whose boundaries or essences are not now, and perhaps never will be, definitively established.[34] The "solipsistic" symptoms and patients I analyze do not constitute some small set of exceptional or anomalous cases, however: they have generally been taken to be central examples or expressions of schizophrenia. Since my use of the term "schizophrenia" focuses on the symptomatic picture rather than the course of illness, it is more consistent with the classic writings of the psychiatrists Eugen Bleuler, Karl Jaspers, and Kurt Schneider than with those of Emil Kraepelin.[35] But my main concern is not nosological or diagnostic in nature. I am primarily seeking a better understanding of particular forms of consciousness or modes of experience. Though particularly common in patients traditionally thought of as schizophrenic, these can also be found, in milder or attenuated form, in other persons—perhaps, to a very limited extent, in all of us but especially in persons having what is called the "schizophrenia spectrum" of disorders (which includes, in addition to schizophrenia proper, the schizoaffective and schizophreniform types of illness and schizotypal and schizoid personality types).[36]

I also recognize the improbability that all the symptoms of any one schizophrenic (or, indeed, of any individual) can be understood in a single way—for example, as expressions of a certain existential orientation or "world design" such as solipsism. Anyone familiar with schizophrenic patients, with the vast literature about them, or with Schreber's endlessly convoluted *Memoirs* will certainly suspect that there are more things in this strange disease than are likely to be dreamed of in any philosophy, even one as peculiar as solipsism or as complex and wide-ranging as Wittgenstein's. Thus, I do not wish to imply that no aspect or moment of Schreber's experience should be seen as inconsistent with the solipsistic interpretation. He may at times manifest what might appropriately be termed poor reality-testing (though much less frequently than is usually supposed; but see M, 223). The present study is, therefore, a kind of thought experiment—not an essentialistic set of claims but an exploratory attempt to see just how many aspects of schizophrenic-type pathology can be understood on the solipsistic reading.[37]

In this book, I do not preoccupy myself with the limitations of my Wittgensteinian reading, with specifying just which patients or symptoms do, and which do not, fit my interpretation. It would, in my view, be premature to attempt to specify in any precise, independent fashion the domain to which my description applies.[38] Indeed, the only way to stake out this domain may be to say the following: the patients and symptoms I am trying to describe are precisely those patients and symptoms who fit my description. Though this may sound outrageously circular, it is almost inevitable in a work whose goal, as Wittgenstein might have put it, is not to describe an already demarcated territory (such as an already recognized schizophrenic subtype or a symptom whose definition is already established) so much as to draw our conceptual map of psychopathology in a somewhat new way.[39] I hope that, in addition to revealing deeper and more coherent patterns in many schizophrenic-type illnesses, and to accounting for phenomena that remain otherwise unexplained, my approach also suggests new questions and opens up new ways of thinking about psychopathology.

1

A MIND'S EYE WORLD

People who do nothing feel responsible for everything.

—Jean-Paul Sartre, *Les Séquestrés d'Altona*

Before proceeding to my main concern, the interpretation of Schreber's delusions in the light of Wittgenstein's thought, we must first consider in greater depth two issues only sketched in the introduction: the nature of traditional views of delusion and poor reality-testing, and the characteristics of schizophrenic illness which appear to call these views into question.

REALITY TESTING AND REGRESSION

In the most recent diagnostic systems of the American Psychiatric Association, *DSM-III* and *DSM-III-R* (instituted in 1980 and 1987, and now influential throughout much of the world), "delusion" is defined as a "false personal belief based on incorrect inference about external reality and firmly sustained in spite of what almost everyone else believes and in spite of what constitutes incontrovertible and obvious proof or evidence to the contrary." A "bizarre delusion" is defined as "a false belief whose content is patently absurd and has no possible basis in fact," or as "a false belief that involves a phenomenon that the person's culture would regard as totally implausible."[1] The express purpose of these diagnostic systems is to be as atheoretical as possible, to base diagnosis on unambiguous and publicly observable criteria that require a minimum of interpretation or judgment. In fact, however, their official vocabularies of description (like all such vocabularies) are fraught with theoretical baggage.

Such terms as "false," "incorrect," and "absurd" are obviously value-laden, and they implicitly invoke a particular context or form of life (what in phenomenological and hermeneutic writing might be called a horizon of experience). They treat the patient's assertions as (failed) attempts to refer to the kind of external reality to which normal canons of obvious proof or evidence and consensual agreement apply. In this way they imply that, in some crucial sense, patients have the subjective experience of living in the same kind of commonsense world as the rest of us—it is just that they are in error, a fact apparent from the standpoint of the external observer. The very familiarity to us of this commonsense form of life in which we take the existence of the external world for granted—the philosopher Edmund Husserl called it the "natural attitude"—may account for why mental health professionals so readily adopt, and then so easily forget, the normalizing assumptions implicit in what seem to be merely behavioral criteria for defining madness. There is something both comfortable and compelling about a formulation that assimilates the different to the familiar, thus not overstraining our capacity for imaginative empathy.

Delusions have also been assimilated to familiar modes of experience through being interpreted as unusually intense but essentially normal wish-fulfillment fantasies that are entertained in a state of diminished critical judgment. In his famous "Autistic Thinking" (1912), Eugen Bleuler compared the schizophrenic's delusions to the dream of a youngster playing general on a hobbyhorse or the fantasies of a poet in love: "All these," he wrote, "are but points along the same scale."[2] Valerio, a character in Georg Büchner's *Leonce and Lena*, a play written in the 1830s, expresses most vividly this normalizing, wish-fulfillment vision of the motives and methods of madness, this view of delusion as replacing reality with belief in a brighter and more satisfying world:

> That would be something. A madman! A madman! Who'll exchange his madness for my reason?—Ha, I'm Alexander the Great! How the sun

> shines a golden crown into my hair, how my uniform sparkles. Generalissimo Grasshopper, assemble the troops. Lord Spider, my Minister of Finance, I need more money. Dear Lady-in-waiting Dragonfly, how is my cherished consort, the Empress Beanstalk? Oh, my most excellent physician in ordinary, Dr. Cantharides, I am in need of a son and heir. And on top of these delicious fantasies you get good soup, good meat, good bread, a good bed to sleep on and your hair cut for nothing—in the madhouse, I mean.[3]

In psychoanalysis, the poor reality-testing and wish-fulfillment notions are conjoined and subsumed under the concept of developmental primitivity. In accordance with the Freudian regression/fixation model of psychopathology, schizophrenic and other psychotic delusions are interpreted as pathological revivals of the "original infantile story"—a magical form of experience dominated by hallucinatory wish fulfillment, by "diminished capacity to reflect on the self and on immediate experience," and by inability to distinguish the real from the imaginary.[4] According to this conception, the schizophrenic is like the child of age five or younger to whom everything seems real.[5] Indeed, in the view of Harold Searles,

> the deeply schizophrenic individual has, subjectively, no imagination. The moment that something which *we* would call a new concoction of fantasy, a new product of his imagination, enters his awareness, *he* perceives this as being an actual and undisguised attribute of the world around him. He cannot yet experience a realm of the imagination, differentiated as such, demarcated from the realm of perception of real events round about. Similarly, memories of past events are experienced by him not as such, but rather as literal reenactments.

Searles, who might himself be accused of taking his psychotic informants rather too literally, describes schizophrenics as showing "the persistent conviction that people can quite literally be turned into trees or animals or buildings or rocks, and vice versa"[6]

According to this model of schizophrenia, unmodulated desires and the wild meanderings of primary-process thought overwhelm logic, the capacity for reflective distance from experience, and all sense of realism and social convention.[7] This widely accepted image is well conveyed by the psychoanalyst Marguerite Sechehaye's description of an essentially Dionysian illness—schizophrenia as the triumph of the passions: "Freed of social control, stripped of logical and moral imperatives, deprived of conscious directives, [schizophrenic thinking] sends its roots to the very heart of the desires, the dreads and the fundamental drives of which it is the cherished instrument of expression. Invested with an affective potential drawn from reality, it charges the inanimate world of objects with life, energy and the strength of the drives from which it emanates."[8]

The view taken by many in the radical antipsychiatry movement is surprisingly similar—differing only in its positive rather than negative evaluation of this supposedly Dionysian state of regression. Thus, in Deleuze and Guattari's influential *Anti-Oedipus: Capitalism and Schizophrenia*, "schizophrenia [is] defined loosely, and not clinically, as the uncontrollable, polymorphous movement of desire emanating from within the social production."[9] Such a vision of the schizophrenic is also remarkably close to the evolutionist image of tribal or primitive man that once prevailed in cultural anthropology—a being described by Bronislaw Malinowski and Claude Lévi-Strauss (both vigorous opponents of such a view) as "lawless, inhuman, and savage," a "creature barely emerged from an animal condition and still a prey to his needs and instincts," a "consciousness governed by emotions and lost in a maze of confusion and [magical] participation."[10] In all these cases, madness is imagined as something wild and dark, a place of unfathomable mystery and uncontrollable passions existing beyond the confines of civilized life.

ANOMALOUS FEATURES OF SCHIZOPHRENIC EXPERIENCE AND BEHAVIOR

Oddly enough, certain prominent characteristics of many schizophrenic patients do not seem to be consistent either with the notion of poor reality-testing as a failure of the ego or with the interpretation of delusions as involving regression to an infantile or Dionysian state. Let us consider these anomalous features, features that seem to imply the presence of something deeply contradictory in the schizophrenic condition.

First, it is difficult to square standard notions of poor reality-testing with the fact that many schizophrenics who seem to be profoundly preoccupied with their delusions, and who cannot be swayed from belief in them, nevertheless treat these same beliefs with what seems a certain distance or irony. I mentioned above a patient who stated that his own delusions seemed rather fantastic.[11] The eminent psychiatrist Manfred Bleuler (the son of Eugen) has remarked on the significance of "the smile of schizophrenics" which "has been accorded too little attention": "Schizophrenics can smile in a soulful, expressive way. Their smile," he believes, "tells us something like: 'Dear friend, it's all just an act. Somehow, in some other world, we'll get along with one another.'"[12] One of Eugen Bleuler's patients was well aware that the voices he heard originated in his own ears, for he compared these voices to the sound of the sea that can be heard by placing a shell to one's ear.[13] It seems that something about the hallucinations and delusions of such patients sets their delusional worlds apart from the realm of normal, consensual reality.

A related feature of schizophrenic patients is what has been called their "double bookkeeping." It is remarkable to what extent even the most disturbed schizophrenics may retain, even at the height of their psychotic periods, a quite accurate sense of what would generally be considered to be their objective or actual circumstances. Rather than mistaking the imaginary for the real, they often seem to live in two parallel but separate worlds: consensual reality and the realm of their hallucinations and delusions. A patient who claims that the doctors and nurses are trying to torture and poison her may nevertheless happily consume the food they give her; a patient who asserts that the people around him are phantoms or automatons still interacts with them as if they were real.[14]

A third characteristic that seems inconsistent with standard conceptions of poor reality-testing concerns the content of schizophrenic delusions. The delusional world described by Bleuler in his article on autistic thinking (and by Büchner in the passage from *Leonce and Lena* quoted above) evokes a realm which, though brighter and more satisfying than the everyday world, is still relatively close to that of normal human life and therefore fairly easy for the normal person to imagine. This is also true of the movie *I Never Promised You a Rose Garden,* in which the hallucinations and delusions involve exaggerations of normal fears, dreams, and wish-fulfillment fantasies. In reality, however, the delusions and hallucinations recognized as being the most characteristic of actual schizophrenics do not simply exaggerate but fundamentally distort, contradict, or call into question the normal human form of life. Indeed, one of the reasons schizophrenic experience can be so difficult to describe or imagine is that it may involve fundamental transformations in the very structures of space, time, and identity, or in the nature and reality of human consciousness itself.

Perhaps the best examples of such distortions are found in the so-called first-rank symptoms of schizophrenia, a set of specific hallucinations and delusions that the psychiatrist Kurt Schneider, a disciple of Jaspers, believed to be especially characteristic of schizophrenic patients.[15] The first-rank symptoms include various hallucinations or delusions in which patients lose a normal sense of owning or controlling their actions, sensations, or thoughts—as when patients feel that all their inner experiences are under the control or scrutiny of some other being, or even that someone other than themselves is actually thinking their thoughts or looking out through their very eyes. "Then I realized why I was studying his face so closely," writes Barbara O'Brien in *Operators and Things*, an autobiographical account of her schizophrenic illness. "Hinton was tuned in on my mind and was studying the analyst's face through my eyes."[16] Schizophrenic patients may also believe, for instance, that what appear to be other human beings are really phantoms or cleverly designed machines quite devoid of any real consciousness, or that the entire universe is responding to each peristaltic movement of their intestines. Jaspers speaks of "metaphysical delusions" that reflect experience of a shattering of the self, or a sense that the universe itself is in some imminent danger or has even ceased to exist.[17] Schizophrenics may believe that they have invented everything they encounter—that, for example, they themselves have invented the story they have just read. One patient claimed that he used to be a drawing in a book but had finally escaped and come to the hospital. Another declared that he contained within his own body all the heavenly bodies while also maintaining that these heavenly bodies simultaneously existed in the outer world.[18] Such delusions are not explicable as wish-fulfillment fantasies—at least not readily so—for even if they do, at some level, involve intense wishes, the wishes themselves seem in need of considerable elucidation before they can be empathically understood or can play an explanatory role.

Nor is the characteristic tone or atmosphere of many such delusions consistent with the psychoanalytic interpretation of regression to a primitive or Dionysian form of consciousness. For one thing, the famous "flat affect" observed in so many schizophrenics, as well as the devitalized and derealized quality that often permeates their experiential world, hardly suggests a regressed state charged with the energy and vitality of the primary process. According to Eugen Bleuler, "schizophrenics can write whole autobiographies without manifesting the least bit of emotion. They will describe their suffering and their actions as if it were a theme in physics."[19] Here is how one schizoaffective patient describes the unreality feeling that plagued her during much of her psychosis:

> It is more like gray. It is like a constant sliding and shifting that slips away in a jelly-like fashion, leaving nothing substantial and yet enough to be tasted, or like watching a movie based on a play and, having once seen the play, realizing that the movie is a description of it and one that brings back memories and yet isn't real. . . . Even a description of it is unreal and tormenting, for it is horrifying and yet seems mild and vague, although it is acute. It is felt in an unreal way in that it isn't constant torture and yet never seems to leave and everything seems to slip away into impressions. . . . For what is, is, and yet what seems to be is always changing and drifting away into thought and ideas, rather than actualities. The important things have left and the unimportant stay behind, making the loss only more apparent by their presence.[20]

Similarly, the schizophrenic patient Renée, in her *Autobiography of a Schizophrenic Girl,* speaks of "the pasteboard scenery of Unreality" during her psychosis, saying "even the sea disappointed me a little by its artificiality." The psychoanalyst Paul Federn describes this state of estrangement as one in which "the world appears substantially unaltered, but yet different: not so spontaneously, so actually, near or far; not clear, warm, friendly, and familiar, not really and truly existing and alive, more as if in a dream and yet different from a dream." Although there is no decline in the ability to think, reason, or perceive, the patient nevertheless senses that "his feeling, wishing, thinking, and memory processes have become different, uncertain, intolerably changed." He may perceive both the external world and the existence of his own ego, but he no longer *feels* their reality; what Pierre Janet called "le sentiment du réel" is lacking.[21]

Along with what might be called these illusions of inauthenticity, which seem to be largely a matter of mood or feeling tone, are more cognitive symptoms that might be termed delusions of disbelief. It has not in fact been sufficiently noted how often schizophrenic delusions involve not belief in the unreal but disbelief in something that most people take to be true. Schizophrenic patients may, for example, speak disbelievingly of "my so-called children and the so-called hospital"; of "a place *called* the laundry, patients *called* us, a woman *called* her, a wreck *called* Emily"; or, in Schreber's case, of the "supposed patients" and a gentleman "who was supposed to be the Medical Director of the Institute" (M, 104–5).[22] In an autobiographical account of his psychosis, Jonathan Lang, a schizophrenic with paranoid and catatonic features, describes several phases of auditory hallucination. In some of these, his voices presented "delusional" content in an explicitly hypothetical or tentative fashion. Thus, during the period he calls "pragmatic spiritualism," which lasted for a few months, the "hallucinating agent . . . presented a group of ideas concerning spiritualism not so much as revelations of an absolute actuality as concepts pragmatically valuable to humans. The concepts were presented allegedly because of their value in bringing affective tone to humans whose lives might otherwise lack it by their promise of an improved future in an after life."[23]

Also accompanying this feeling of lack of reality may be a strange, and seemingly contradictory, quality that R. D. Laing once termed "a kind of phantom concreteness."[24] Despite being felt by the patient to be unreal, schizophrenic delusions and hallucinations are often elaborated with a remarkable degree of detail and specificity and with a certain quality of perceptual concreteness that rivals that of the real world (even though the patient does not usually confuse them with reality).

Given the prominence of these anomalous aspects of schizophrenic experience and behavior, one might expect that standard conceptualizations of schizophrenic delusion would often have been called into question. Actually, the vast majority of psychoanalysts, psychiatrists, and clinical psychologists seem to take it for granted that delusions and hallucinations involve the patient's failure to recognize the subjective nature of his or her idiosyncratic beliefs and perceptions. And, in contemporary psychoanalytic theory, the schizophrenic's supposed incapacity for reality-testing is nearly always assumed to indicate regression to archaic modes of feeling, thought, and perception—to reflect the wish-fulfillment fantasies or states of quasi-mystic union of an infantile mind. But, given the anomalous features discussed above, one might well ask if any other interpretation is possible. Is there an alternative way of understanding schizophrenic delusions which might better capture their phenomenological peculiarities? Or is one forced just to accept, as did Jaspers, the unbridgeable alienness of the schizophrenic world? To answer this question, let us now turn to the experiences recounted in Schreber's memoirs.

SCHREBER'S "SO-CALLED DELUSIONS"

Schreber's *Memoirs of my Nervous Illness* is a remarkable book, a disorienting combination of tentativeness and certitude, of reasonableness and proselytizing zeal. With unfailing lucidity Schreber describes a convoluted, nearly unimaginable world of "nerves," "rays," and "gods," of incessant inner voices and strange compulsions. He speaks, for example, of undergoing a transformation of sex, of losing his stomach, of seeing people change their heads, and of realizing that foreign beings are occupying his consciousness and sometimes controlling the direction of his gaze. Whether, or in what way, Schreber can be said to have believed in these strange phenomena is the difficult question to which I now turn—first by considering a central delusion of Schreber's psychosis, his "belief" that he is being transformed into a woman: "When the rays approach," writes Schreber, referring to the strange, scrutinizing entities—rays—which constitute an important center of consciousness in his delusional world, "my breast gives the impression [*Eindruck*] of a pretty well-developed female bosom." He continues

> this phenomenon [*Erscheinung*] can be *seen* by anybody who wants to

> observe me *with his own eyes* . . . A brief glance however would not suffice, the observer would have to go to the trouble of spending 10 or 15 minutes near me. In that way anybody would notice the periodic swelling and diminution of my bosom. Naturally hairs remain under my arms and on my chest; these are by the way sparse in my case; my nipples also remain small as in the male sex. Notwithstanding, I venture to assert flatly that anybody who sees me standing in front of a mirror with the upper part of my body naked would get the undoubted *impression of a female trunk*—especially when the illusion [*Illusion*] is strengthened by some feminine adornments. (M, 207)[25]

A careful reading of this passage makes it clear that Schreber is not describing a delusion as that term is generally used in accordance with the poor reality-testing formula. He does not claim that there has been any actual anatomical change in his torso, only that under certain circumstances his breast "gives the impression" of being a female bosom. Schreber even takes care to emphasize that the amount of hair and size of his nipples remains as before, and he refers to the impression of femininity as an illusion. Now, it hardly seems surprising that a person preoccupied with the question of whether a torso might conceivably look feminine will, if he continues to stare long enough, be able at moments to experience it in this way, especially when feminine adornments contribute to the impression. Elsewhere in the *Memoirs*, Schreber refers to having to shave off a moustache "to support my imagination of being a female, . . . a moustache would naturally have been an insurmountable obstacle for this *illusion*" (M, 160, emphasis added).[26] These are not atypical examples.

In another passage Schreber describes "picturing," the process in which what he calls "representing" occurs as a volitional and self-aware process:

> To picture [*das Zeichnen*] (in the sense of the soul-language) is the conscious use of the human imagination for the purpose of producing pictures [*Bilder*] (predominantly pictures of recollections) in one's head, which can then be looked at by rays. By vivid imagination I can produce pictures of all recollections from my life, of persons, animals and plants, of all sorts of objects in nature and objects of daily use, so that these

> images become visible either inside my head or if I wish, outside, where I want them to be seen by my own nerves and by the rays. I can do the same with weather phenomena and other events; I can for example let it rain or let lightning strike—this is a particularly effective form of "picturing" [*Zeichnung*], because the weather and particularly lightning are considered by the rays manifestations of the divine gift of miracles; I can also let a house go up in smoke under the window of my flat, etc. (M, 180–81)

But Schreber immediately goes on to say this:

> All this naturally only in my imagination [*Vorstellung*], but in a manner that the rays get the impression that these objects and phenomena really exist. I can also "picture" myself [*mich selbst . . . "zeichnen"*] in a different place, for instance while playing the piano I see myself at the same time standing in front of a mirror in the adjoining room in female attire; when I am lying in bed at night I can give myself and the rays the impression that my body has female breasts and a female sexual organ. (M, 181)

Sometimes, then, the representing is felt to be actively carried out by the self; though at other times—as in the previous passage concerning the impression of a female trunk—it seems to be passively undergone. In both cases, however, Schreber's delusions lack the literalness schizophrenic delusions are so often asssumed to have. He does not make claims about actual characteristics of the objective, external, or consensual world—the sort of statements that could be proved false by referring to evidence independent of the experiences in question.[27] Thus, when Schreber describes a delusional belief about himself, he typically does not say "I am a scoffer at God" or "I am given to voluptuous excesses" but, rather, I am *"represented"* (*dargestellt*) as one of these things (M, 120, also 55, 172). In one passage he even talks about the "lower God" who "create(s) by 'representing' the impression of a person bellowing because he is demented" (M, 166).[28] Such modes of expression suggest that Schreber's delusional experiences retain for him what might be called a "coefficient of subjectivity," as if whatever is experienced has an aura that labels it not as reality but as only an experience. The experiential objects of this mode of experience seem to be recognized as phenomenal in the sense of being encompassed by, or dependent for their existence on, some consciousness that conceives or perceives them. They exist not in a public or objective realm but only, as Schreber often puts it, "in the mind's eye" (e.g., M, 109, 117n, 124, 137, 181–82, 227).

Schreber, it seems, is well aware of the difficulty of communicating the specific quality of such a lived-world to people who have not had such experiences themselves: "Again it is extremely difficult to describe these changes in words because matters are dealt with which lack all analogies in human experience and which I appreciated directly only in part with my mind's eye [*mit meinem geistigen Auge*]" (M, 117). It is understandable, therefore, that he should describe his delusions and hallucinations in what his translators call "involved and endless sentences contain[ing] clauses within clauses" (M, 26). As Schreber puts it, "To make myself at least somewhat comprehensible I shall have to speak much in images and similes, which may at times perhaps be only *approximately* correct" (M, 41).

The tentative, nonliteral, and self-aware quality of Schreber's assertions is even more apparent in the original German. As the translators state in their introduction, they omitted many frequently used phrases and particles that would have been translated in English as "in part," "on the other hand," "so to speak," "up to a point," and "in a way." The translators felt that such phrases should be excised since they were awkward and did "not add to the sense" (M, 26). This would seem a reasonable enough decision if one were primarily concerned with the content of Schreber's delusional or quasi-delusional world. If, however, it is the form of the patient's world that one wishes to grasp, the excised phrases take on great significance, for they alter the whole tone of the text and the nature of its claims. Notice that all the phrases in question appear to involve qualifications by Schreber of potential literal implications of his text or warnings to readers not to assimilate what they read to their own, more normal mode of experience. At the very least, these phrases mitigate the absolute egocentricity, dogmatism, and literalism so readily ascribed to a psychotic world like Schreber's.

Schreber's perception of himself as feminine appears, in fact, to be an example of a fairly common, but philosophically problematic, perceptual experience to which Wittgenstein devoted considerable attention—what the philosopher calls "seeing-as" or "aspect seeing." "Seeing-as" refers to that occurrence of a "change of aspect" in which one has the experience "of a *new* perception and at the same time of the perception's being unchanged": "I contemplate a face, and then suddenly notice its likeness to another. I *see* that it has not changed; and yet I see it differently. I call this experience 'noticing an aspect'." (PI, 196, 193).

In the *Philosophical Investigations*, Wittgenstein points out that, given standard ways of conceiving experience, seeing-as is a kind of hybrid phenomenon; it can equally well—or equally inappropriately—be described as a perceptual or as a conceptual process: "Hence the flashing of an aspect on us seems half visual experience, half thought. . . . 'But this isn't *seeing*!'—'But this is seeing!'—It must be possible to give both remarks a conceptual justification" (PI, 197, 203). The aspect that flashes does appear out there as a feature of the perceived world, and it can loom up spontaneously, like a perception. But, unlike more normal or habitual acts of perceptual recognition (e.g., recognizing a fork as a fork; PI, 195), seeing-as often involves some reflexive awareness of the role played by the attitude one takes toward the perceptual object (PI, 204–5). Also, in seeing-as the aspect seen may be experienced as something added onto, or coexisting with, some more fundamental percept.[29]

Another distinctive feature Wittgenstein describes is the fact that seeing-as can be affected or brought about by acts of will, something that is not characteristic of standard acts of seeing. Thus, it is reasonable to try to see a given aspect, just as it is reasonable to try to imagine a mental image of something. Wittgenstein: "One wants to ask of seeing an aspect. 'Is it seeing? Is it thinking?' The aspect is subject to the will; this by itself relates it to thinking" (RPPII, 544). Wittgenstein's point is not that seeing-as always responds to our will, or never changes against our will, but that to attempt to see a given aspect is an action that is not incoherent or illogical, and one that can at times be successful. (Think, for example, of the subtle mix of willful and spontaneous factors as one looks at the famous duck-rabbit or vase-face pictures and tries to bring about the Gestalt shifts.) As Wittgenstein says, "It makes sense to say [of seeing-as],

'See this circle as a hole, not as a disc,' but it doesn't make sense to say [of standard acts of perception], 'See it as a rectangle,' 'See it as being red'" (RPPII, 545).[30]

Schreber's experience of being represented as a woman seems to have these same qualities. As we have seen, he does have some control over the feminization, since he can, at least at times, bring it on by staring at himself in his feminine adornments while concentrating on the question of his own femininity. Also, he experiences the female aspect of his physical appearance as overlaying something more fundamental, his basically masculine anatomy. Indeed, he himself defines what he calls "the notion of 'representing'" as "giving to a thing or a person a semblance different from its real nature (expressed in human terms 'of falsifying')" (M, 120).[31] It is clear from many parts of the *Memoirs*, however, that Schreber does not consider representing to be *mere* falsifying, since he takes what is represented in the mind's eye—for instance, his own feminization—very seriously and even considers it at times to be the manifestation of a deeper and somehow more significant reality.

In *Dementia Praecox or the Group of Schizophrenias*, Eugen Bleuler suggests that the seeming confusions of identity so characteristic of schizophrenics may involve a similar kind of awareness and should therefore not be taken too literally. The patients he describes certainly seem to have at least a partial awareness of engaging in a kind of seeing-as:

> If a patient says the doctor is Count N., this confusion of persons should not be understood in the sense of a normal individual confusing persons. Patients will assume the presence of real or imaginary people in accordance with the momentary situation. A woman patient wishes to strike me because I am her acquaintance, Mr. R. When I protest, she says, "Don't come here as R. Come at least as O. or P." ("No, I prefer to come as M.") "You can't possibly be that person. He is an angel, a god . . . ." A patient is very rude to a lady visitor. However, the patient claims that while she certainly cursed that woman, it was not aimed at her personally and should not be held against the patient.[32]

It would be idle, Wittgenstein suggests, to argue over whether such an experience—"the flashing of an aspect"—can be considered an event or act of seeing: it is both like and unlike what might be considered paradigm cases of seeing, such as the perception of a fork as a fork. But, clearly, if one did choose to call an instance of seeing-as an act of seeing, it would be important not to forget how it differs from the paradigm instances of seeing. Those who uncritically accept the poor reality-testing definition of a hallucination as "a perception without an object" seem to make just this error, that of assimilating seeing-as to standard cases of perceiving.

Yet it would be equally mistaken to think of an instance of seeing-as as being merely interpretive or imaginary, thereby assimilating it to a conceptual process. After all, as we have noted, seeing-as does have some of the phenomenological qualities of standard acts of perception. Also, seeing-as remains faithful to certain qualities of the stimulus object, with its interpretive freedom operating in a fairly restricted domain (thus, the interpretations characteristic of seeing-as are less likely to affect more perceptual qualities of an item seen, such as its color or shape).[33] In similar fashion, Schreber's perception of his own feminine aspect does not distort or deny the more objective qualities of the perceptual world: the very presence of hair on his chest and the size of his nipples is unaffected; only the prominence or meaning attributed to these parts of his anatomy is altered in the context of the feminizing seeing-as.

The medical examiner, Dr. Weber, states that Schreber's delusions and hallucinations involve "unshakable certainty and adequate motive for action." In his expert report he describes Schreber as having "real hallucinations," whose "characteristic [is] that they are taken for factual and real and have the same acuity as other sensations" (M, 320). Schreber insists, however, that such beliefs—he calls them "my so-called delusions"—refer to a separate realm, one that does not motivate him to act and wherein the usual criteria of worldly proof or belief do not apply. In such passages as the following, written by Schreber in response to Dr. Weber's report and appended to the *Memoirs*, Schreber quite explicitly denies the usual implications of a poor reality-testing interpretation. The combination of incorrigibility and inconsequentiality Jaspers describes could hardly be stated more clearly:

I have to confirm the first part (a) of this [Dr. Weber's] statement, namely that my so-called delusional system is unshakable certainty, with the same decisive *"yes"* as I have to counter the second part (b), namely that my delusions are adequate motive for action, with the strongest possible *"no."* I could even say with Jesus Christ: "My Kingdom is not of this world"; my so-called delusions are concerned solely with God and the beyond; they *can* therefore *never in any way influence my behavior* in any worldly matter, if I may use this expression—apart from the whim already mentioned, which is also meant to impress God [the whim Schreber refers to is his habit of standing in front of the mirror with feminine adornments]. I do not know how the medical expert arrived at the contrary conclusion, namely that my delusions are sufficient motive for action; at least I do not think I have given any grounds for this belief either in my behavior or in the written expositions of my "Memoirs." . . . I have no intention whatever as the medical examiner imputed . . . to make pecuniary sacrifices to propagate my belief in miracles, to have the nerves of voluptuousness in my body verified or to increase the "material well-being" which rests on them. Whoever thinks this is possible has not really entered into my inner spiritual life; but naturally I do not intend any reproach with this statement, because a full understanding is really impossible for other people. The certainty of my knowledge of God and divine matters is so great and unshakable that it is completely immaterial to me what other people think of the truth or probability of my ideas. I shall therefore—other than for the purpose of this legal action—never undertake anything by way of spreading my experiences and beliefs among people except publishing my Memoirs." (M, 301–2)[34]

That Schreber's claims were in large measure true is confirmed by the judge's assessment of the situation:

Dr. Weber confirms that plaintiff [Schreber] never carried out *any unreasonable or incorrect action, . . . always acted cautiously and sensibly, taking into consideration all the circumstances. . . .* In short, in the whole of plaintiff's behaviour during his contact with the world outside the Asylum, there has until now *not been a single fact* which could give well-founded grounds for anxiety, that the patient would allow himself to be led astray under the compulsion of his delusional system. (M, 349)

We see, then, that Schreber's delusions did not necessarily involve mistaking the imaginary for the real. They could, however, involve the converse: much of the time Schreber maintained a belief in the *unreality* of virtually everything and every person he saw around him, even when these were in fact objectively real:

> Having lived for months among miracles, I was inclined to take more or less everything I saw for a miracle. Accordingly I did not know whether to take the streets of Leipzig through which I traveled as only theatre props, perhaps in the fashion in which Prince Potemkin is said to have put them up for Empress Catherine II of Russia during her travels through the desolate country, so as to give her the impression of a flourishing countryside. At Dresden Station, it is true, I saw a fair number of people who *gave the impression* [*Eindruck*] of being railway passengers. (M, 102, emphasis added)

At times Schreber was convinced that all the people he saw had been "miracled up" or "fleetingly improvised" by rays in order to deceive him, and that, rather than having a separate existence in themselves, they appeared and disappeared like pictures (M, 43n, 102–7, 148). One of his psychiatrists reports that Schreber told him "that the world had come to an end, that everything he saw round himself was only sham, he himself and the persons around him only lifeless shadows" (M, 269). According to a medical report, Schreber "apparently thought he was in another world. At least he considered everything around him to be spirits, taking his environment to be a world of illusions" (M, xxi).

In another remarkable passage, Schreber describes himself as sitting in a park where wasps or other insects repeatedly appear before his eyes (M, 185–88). He was convinced that these apparent insects were brought into being at the very instant his eyes fell on them, and that they disappeared when he looked away. During this experience, which he called "the wasp miracle" (M, 233), these creatures seem to have felt to him like things that existed only when he experienced them, and solely for the purpose of being seen by him. What would to the normal person have the quality of reality—existence independent of that of the self-as-subject—seems to have had for Schreber the ephemeral quality of something merely phenomenal. And it seems that this feeling could apply rather generally, to the world rather than merely to a few objects within the world: as Schreber explains in another passage, for two years "I had to assume and was forced by my experiences to assume [that] all creation on earth would have to perish with the exception of some play-with-miracles in my immediate surroundings" (M, 60).

Clearly, neither Schreber's "so-called delusions" nor his delusions of disbelief are consistent with the standard poor reality-testing formula: in neither case is an objectively inaccurate perception or belief held by the patient to be real. Although Schreber certainly does consider his delusions to be of profound importance (in this limited sense one might say that they have a certain reality), he nevertheless experiences them as pervaded by some quality of subjectivization, as if he were experiencing not objective entities but only appearances or representations.

WITTGENSTEIN ON SOLIPSISM

"The world is *my* world"; "the world is my idea": these were Wittgenstein's succinct statements of the central intuition of the metaphysical vision of the solipsist.[35] It is a vision of reality as a dream, but with awareness of the fact that one is dreaming. For the solipsist, other people, other seeming centers of consciousness, are but dream personages, figments of the solipsist's own conscious activity and awareness.[36] Wittgenstein speaks of solipsism as "a serious and deep-seated disease of language (one might also say 'of thought')" (NFL, 309), a metaphysical illness to which he himself had been, and perhaps remained, susceptible.

In what frame of mind must one be, asks Wittgenstein, in order to feel profoundly struck with the truth of notions such as that "the world is my world" or that "only I feel real pain" or "really see (or hear)"? Or, to put the question differently, what is the sort of experience of the world to which this doctrine might correspond, out of which it is likely to arise? As is typical of Wittgenstein, he does not concern himself with the truth or falsity of solipsism as a metaphysical doctrine. He wants to wean philosophy from idle speculation about these kinds of unanswerable issues and to move it toward more useful questions that will allow people to dissolve such metaphysical conjectures or worries. One method of doing this is to consider what might be called the experiential counterpart to the metaphysical doctrine—that is, the mode of existence that supports the doctrine, whether by motivating or by justifying it. (One might think of this as a contextualizing, a phenomenologizing, or even a psychologizing of metaphysics.)[37]

Wittgenstein mentions two aspects of the experiential stance corresponding to solipsism. The first is absence of activity:

> To get clear about philosophical problems, it is useful to become conscious of the apparently unimportant details of the particular situation in which we are inclined to make a certain metaphysical assertion. Thus we may be tempted to say 'Only this is really seen' when we stare at unchanging surroundings, whereas we may not at all be tempted to say this when we look about us while walking. (BBB, 66)

The second aspect is an abnormal intensity of one's way of looking:

> The phenomenon of *staring* is closely bound up with the whole puzzle of solipsism. (NFL, 309)

> Ask yourself: what does the word 'feeling', or still better 'experience', make you concentrate on? What is it like to concentrate on experience? If *I* try to do this I, e.g., open my eyes particularly wide and stare. (NFL, 315)

> By attending, looking, you produce the impression; you can't look at the impression. (BBB, 176)

Moving about the world, one is forced to observe the multifacetedness of objects and thus to recognize that their total being can never be captured by their phenomenal appearance at any given moment. By interacting with the world—for example, by picking up an object—one is obliged to recognize the world's otherness. The very weight of the object and the resistance it offers to the hand testify to its existence as something independent of will or consciousness. Yet the act of moving a physical object also confirms one's own experience of activity and efficacy, thus precluding a sense of passivization as well as subjectivization.[38]

By contrast, in a passive state the world may look rather different.

The more one stares at things, the more they may seem to have a coefficient of subjectivity; the more they may come to seem "things seen." When staring fixedly ahead, the field of consciousness as such can come into prominence; then, it is as if the lens of awareness were clouding over and the world beyond were taking on the diaphanous quality of a dream. At this point a person can be said to experience *experience* rather than the world, to have the impression of seeing not, say, an actual and physical stove but a "visual stove," the stove-as-seen-by-me (to use one of Wittgenstein's examples). Everything, we might say, is felt to be an instance of seeing-as, of an aspect seeing that is in some sense willful and conceptual in nature; but in this case the aspects or interpretations seem to be the only reality there is. In this situation, any object of awareness tends to feel as if it depends on me in some special way, belonging to my consciousness as a private and somehow inner possession. The "bare present image," in Wittgenstein's words, no longer seems "the worthless momentary picture [but] the true world among shadows" (NB, 83).[39]

Under circumstances such as these, the consciousness of other persons can seem only dubious at best, for I can have no direct experience of their experiences but only of their behavior—which could, conceivably, turn out to be that of a mere dream image or an automaton (the famous problem of other minds). Indeed, on the solipsistic hypothesis, the notion that anyone else has personal experience is hardly even meaningful; as Wittgenstein points out, it "transcends all possible experience" (BBB, 48).

This kind of experience, Wittgenstein explains, is not likely to occur when you are interested in some object in the world but, rather, when there is a certain disengagement and introversion—when, as he puts it, "you concentrated on, as it were stared at, your sensations" rather than seeing right through your sensations to a world filled with real objects of interest and use:

> But what can it mean to speak of "turning my attention on to my own consciousness"? This is surely the queerest thing there could be! It was a particular act of gazing that I called doing this. I stared fixedly in front of me—but *not* at any particular point or object. My eyes were wide open, the brows not contracted (as they mostly are when I am interested in a particular object). No such interest preceded this gazing. My glance was

> vacant; or again *like* that of someone admiring the illumination of the sky and drinking in the light. (PI, §412)

SCHREBER AS SOLIPSIST

The circumstances of Schreber's delusional experiences correspond precisely to those which, according to Wittgenstein's analysis, give rise to the metaphysical vision of solipsism. Schreber explains, "I considered absolute passivity almost a religious duty." God seemed to make "the monstrous demand that I should behave continually as if I myself were a corpse." In fact, the very preservation of his own existence, as well as that of God and the universe itself, sometimes seemed to depend on his remaining still (M, 127–29). Accordingly, he spent much time in a state of extreme inactivity:

> Apart from daily morning and afternoon walks in the garden, I mainly sat *motionless* the whole day on a chair at my table, did not even move towards the window, where by the way nothing was to be seen except green trees . . . ; even in the garden I preferred to remain seated always in the same spot, and was only occasionally urged by the attendants to walk about, really against my will." (M, 127)

According to Dr. Weber's expert report, Schreber, this "physically strong man in whom frequent jerkings of the face musculature and marked tremor of the hands were noticeable, was at first completely inaccessible and shut off in himself, lay or stood immobile and stared with frightened eyes straight ahead of himself into space." As was clear, however, "this rigid demeanour was far removed from indifference, rather the patient's whole state seemed tense, irritable, caused by inner uneasiness." And, Dr. Weber claimed, "there could be no doubt that he was continually influenced by vivid and painful hallucinations." Other observers reported that Schreber was often to be seen standing motionless in the garden, staring into the sun and grimacing (M, 268–69; see also 280).

Schreber was also frequently in a state of heightened awareness in which he scrutinized the world, and scrutinized his awareness of the world. Far from demonstrating an incapacity for concentration or self-monitoring, so often ascribed to schizophrenia, he was unable to perform the most trivial act—such as watching a butterfly flutter past—without obsessively reflecting on his own experience and checking on whether he was really doing what he thought he was doing. As the following passage suggests, his hallucinatory voices were often the expression of this self-consciousness:

> It is so obstinately held that I have become stupid to such a degree that day after day one doubts whether I still recognize people around me, whether I still understand ordinary natural phenomena, or articles of daily use . . . indeed even whether I still know *who I am or have been*. The phrase "has been recorded" with which I was examined, follows when my gaze has been directed towards certain things and I have seen them; they are then registered on my nerves with this phrase. [As Schreber has previously explained, the words "has been recorded" mean "recorded into awareness or comprehension."] For example, when I saw the doctor my nerves immediately resounded with "has been recorded," or "the senior attendant—has been recorded," or, "a joint of pork—has been recorded." . . . And all this goes on in endless repetition day after day, hour after hour.
>
> . . . Whenever a butterfly appears my gaze is *first* directed to it as to a being newly created that very moment, and *secondly* the words 'butterfly—has been recorded' are spoken into my nerves by the voices; this shows that one thought I could possibly no longer recognize a butterfly and one therefore examines me to find out whether I still know the meaning of the word 'butterfly'. (M, 188)[40]

The experience of the "miracled-up" insects—this sense of being the conscious center before whom and for whom events appear—seems not to have occurred unless Schreber was in a state of immobility. He explains that if he walked about in the garden the miracle would not happen, but if he sat down and waited he could actually provoke this wasp miracle (M, 233). Such withdrawal from action, especially prominent in catatonic patients, is common in schizophrenia and often seems to be a precondition for the onset of certain symptoms, including auditory and kinesthetic hallucinations and certain profound delusions of reference. According to the schizophrenic patient Jonathan Lang, for example, "withdrawal from sensorimotor activity" into what he called "the ideological level" of abstract thought was the central feature of his own psychotic state.[41]

We have seen how obsessed Schreber was with the need to stare, to scrutinize every passing thought or perception. It is significant that the impression of the feminization of his body occurred at a time when he combined such intense concentration with passivity—that is, when he stood still in front of a mirror staring at himself for an extended period of time. And, as we saw, under these circumstances he did *not* have the sense of watching a literal or objective change come over his body; it was rather the experience of seeing his body as if from a certain point of view, one that, while rendering the body as feminine, was still recognized as a point of view—as, we might say, an instance of seeing-as (though this point of view was accorded a singular importance). Let us call this the attitude of "quasi-solipsism" (since the experience is not accompanied by a full and explicit awareness in philosophical terms of the doctrine of solipsism).

Another prominent aspect of Schreber's delusional experience is also suggestive of the world of the solipsist, and it too occurs in a state of passive hyperconcentration: his encounter with what in philosophy is called the problem of other minds. Inevitably, the solipsist must confront the issue of whether it is possible for other human beings to have consciousness, or whether, unlike the self, they are only things, or even mere images or figments of imagination. The solipsist, who is so struck with the undeniable actuality and centrality of his own experience, obviously cannot have this same awareness of the experience of others. In fact, the more he pays attention to his own experience, the more unlikely it seems that other people can have anything like *this*—and the more others come to seem unbridgeably apart and different, perhaps not really conscious beings at all.[42] Consider the following passage from the *Memoirs*, in which Schreber appears to shift from a quasi-solipsistic attitude (experiencing an ephemeral world of vanishing images) to an awareness of the nonexistence of other minds:

> I have witnessed not once but hundreds of times how human shapes were set down for a short time by divine miracles only to be dissolved again or vanish. The voices talking to me designated these visions the so-called *"fleeting-improvised-men"* [*flüchtig hingemachte Männer*]. . . . all of them were leading a so-called dream life [*ein sog. Traumleben*], i.e. they

> did not give the impression of being capable of holding a sensible conversation, just as I myself was at that time also little inclined to talk, mainly because I thought that I was faced not by real people but by miraculously created puppets. (M, 43n)[43]

In another passage, Schreber recalls engaging in such speculations after a particularly vivid visual experience during which he stared intently at the sunlight (probably while standing still) until it seemed to fill a large part of the sky:

> One of the many things incomprehensible to me is that other human beings should have existed at that time apart from myself, and that the attendant M., who alone accompanied me at the time, remained apparently totally indifferent to this phenomenon [of the sunlight]. But his indifference did not really astonish me, because I considered him a fleeting-improvised-man, who of course led a dream-life and so could not be expected to have any understanding for those impressions which must inspire a thinking human being with the highest interest. (M, 125; see also 59n)[44]

The stance of passive concentration gave rise, then, in perfect accordance with Wittgenstein's analysis of solipsism, to a pervasive sense of subjectivization, of experiencing experience rather than the external world, to a feeling that, as Schreber puts it, "everything that happens is in reference to me" (M, 197), as well as to the characteristic solipsistic experience of the problem of other minds (the feeling that others are merely "fleeting-improvised-men"). Such experiences of delusional and subjectivized reality seem to be embedded in a form of consciousness that is hyperacute, hyper-self-conscious, and highly detached, qualities not at all characteristic of early stages of cognitive-emotional development. For, as William James once suggested, a lived-world that foregrounds awareness of subjectivization and innerness, of the mind's role in constituting the world, would seem to be highly advanced from a cognitive-developmental point of view:

> So far is it from being true that our first way of feeling things is the feeling of them as subjective or mental, that the exact opposite seems rather to

be the truth. Our earliest, most instinctive, least developed kind of consciousness is the objective kind; and only as reflection becomes developed do we become aware of an inner world at all. . . . subjective consciousness, aware of itself as subjective, does not at first exist.[45]

ANOMALOUS FEATURES OF SCHIZOPHRENIA IN THE LIGHT OF SOLIPSISM

Some of the anomalous characteristics of the schizophrenic delusional world can be accounted for as aspects of their quasi-solipsism. Consider, for example, the "specific schizophrenic incorrigibility" of what Schreber calls his "so-called delusions"—with their absolute imperviousness to argument or external proof and their strange, seemingly paradoxical combination of certainty with inconsequentiality. Contrary to Jaspers's view, this feature is not beyond the pale of any possible understanding. Indeed, it is natural that solipsistic claims cannot be refuted or adjudicated in any public domain. The claim that one is represented as a female is not, after all, the sort of statement to which corroborative or disconfirmatory evidence could possibly be relevant. No imaginable fact—not the roughness of a beard, the narrowness of hips, or even the anatomical presence of male genitalia—could possibly refute the fact of the experience of the representing, the occurrence in a private mental space of this image of a body's femininity, this instance of seeing-as. As Wittgenstein often pointed out in his later writings (e.g., PI, §402), it is nonsensical to doubt immediate subjective experience and impossible to argue (at least in any standard manner) about notions like solipsism, since normal forms of evidence are quite irrelevant to such assertions.

Nor is the agreement of others pertinent to an experience which, paradoxically enough, is in one way absolutely private and in another way quite universal (since no one else can share my consciousness, yet my consciousness is All). Others are experienced either as unbridgeably apart or as nonexistent, with sometimes a rapid oscillation between these two alternatives. And, in both these cases, consensual proof and agreement are not relevant. Thus, Schreber claims, "for myself I am *subjectively certain* that my body . . . shows such organs to an extent as only occurs in the female body" (M, 205). Though he realizes that to other people the "miracles" enacted on his body may seem to be "only the product of a pathologically vivid imagination," he insists on the certainty for himself of his own experiential reality: "I can only give the assurance that hardly any memory from my life is more certain than the miracles recounted in this chapter. What can be more definite for a human being than what he has lived through and felt on his own body?" (M, 132). In another passage Schreber speaks of having "had Professor Flechsig's soul [Flechsig was one of his psychiatrists] and most probably his *whole* soul temporarily in my body," in the form of a bundle, as of wadding or cobweb, which had been "thrown into my belly by way of miracle." This, he tells us, "is an actual or *subjectively certain* event from the distinctness of my recollection—whether other people can or cannot believe me" (M, 91).[46] A patient of Eugen Bleuler's seemed to have a similar sense of the irrelevance of objective facts or consensual criteria of truth. When asked if he thought his hallucinations were real, he replied, "Perhaps they are pathological, perhaps they are real." Bleuler remarks: "The question very obviously does not interest him."[47]

At the same time, however, the solipsist may well not act on those indubitable experiences felt to be constituted by his own consciousness alone (the "so-called delusions"). In a solipsistic universe, to act might feel either unnecessary or impossible: unnecessary because external conditions are at the mercy of thought, since the world is idea (one schizophrenic spoke of "purging" his visual field, to make the "ghostly forms crumple up, become as dry as bone, and helpless"[48]); impossible because real action, action in a world able to resist my efforts, cannot occur in a purely mental universe (Schreber said he would not try to harm himself or commit suicide because he believed that even the most serious injuries to his body could not affect him; M, 281). Indeed, as Wittgenstein's discussion of passivity and staring shows, the very looming up of the solipsist's vision depends on inaction; real activity would threaten to dissipate this dream universe, this world in which all that exists, from the heavenly bodies to other people, feels constituted by, dependent for its existence on, one's own subjectivity. It would seem, then, that incorrigibility and inconsequentiality, the simultaneous certainty and practical irrelevance of the delusional world, are in a sense the normal and natural qualities of a solipsistic, dereified universe.

In the "double bookkeeping" of schizophrenia, the two worlds of experience differ according to their felt ontological status. One, experienced as objective, is perceived in the normal fashion. But the other realm is felt by the patient to exist only "in the mind's eye." Schreber explains with his usual, rather disconcerting lucidity:

> I use here the expression "seeing with the mind's eye," which I used before . . . because I cannot find a more suitable one in our human language. We are used to thinking all impressions we receive from the outer world are mediated through the five senses, particularly that all light and sound sensations are mediated through eye and ear. This may be correct in normal circumstances. However, in the case of a human being who like myself has entered into contact with rays and whose head is in consequence so to speak illuminated by rays, this is not all. I receive light and sound sensations which are projected direct on to my *inner* nervous system by the rays; for their reception the external organs of seeing and hearing are not necessary. I see such events even with eyes closed and where sound is concerned would hear them as in the case of the "voices," even if it were possible to seal my ears hermetically against all other sounds. (M, 117)

Bearing this felt innerness in mind, one can understand why auditory hallucinations often have more the quality of something thought than of something heard. And one can comprehend how patients could "hear" the voices of absent people without finding the phenomenon strange.[49]

This quasi-solipsism also helps to account for the affectless, devitalized, or otherwise derealized atmosphere so often characteristic of the schizoid and schizophrenic lived-world. Elena, a young schizophrenic pianist who was a patient of the Italian psychiatrist G. E. Morselli, described herself as being "drawn by something that is stronger than I am" into the "other life" or "other world" of her madness: "I am closer to the soul, to Dante's Paradise in that world," she said, "but I feel removed from life, devoid of emotion, and detached from everything."[50] Such affectless detachment is frequently interpreted as indicating either an "intrinsic emotional blandness" and incapacity for profound emotional experience[51] or a defensively "autistic" turning of attention and interest away from the surrounding social world and toward experiences that could be described as inner—that is, toward one's own ego or toward fantasies unrelated to external reality.[52] But one person who is only too familiar with this lived-world, the schizophrenic patient Jonathan Lang, disputes both these views as too simplistic.

The innerness of the schizophrenic world, according to Lang, is less a matter of the content than of the form of experience: it involves not so much a turning from one kind of object, an external one, toward another, an internal one (whatever that would be), as a shift of attitude or perspective. As Lang puts it in an article about his illness which he wrote for a psychiatric journal, the schizophrenics's withdrawal "is not so much a withdrawal from society as it is a withdrawal from sensorimotor activity. A considerable proportion of his ideological activity is devoted to other humans."[53] Lang also denies that patients like himself are unaware or devoid of emotions. It is just that their concerns with feelings, as with people, are experienced in the context or perspective of what he calls "the ideological domain"—by which he seems to mean a realm in which everything is felt to be *merely* mental or representational.

The schizoaffective patient quoted earlier in this chapter best captured this sense of profound retreat from actuality into a representational realm by comparing her experience to "watching a movie based on a play and, having once seen the play, realizing that the movie is a description of it and one that brings back memories and yet isn't real."[54] A failure to realize that a patient may be describing such a mode of experience can, incidentally, lead to an overly literal interpretation by the therapist, and thus to the mistaken impression that the patient's reality-testing has broken down.[55] This was the case with one of Eugen Bleuler's patients, who insisted that he was blind when he obviously saw perfectly well. "What he meant," explains Bleuler, "was that he did not perceive things 'as reality'."[56]

Perhaps the most eloquent evocations of the characteristically schizophrenic sense of unreality are to be found in the works of Samuel Beckett, in which the protagonists so often have a schizoid orientation and the settings serve as metaphors for their quasi-solipsism. The hero of *Murphy*, for instance, pictures his mind "as a large hollow sphere, hermetically closed to the universe without. This was not an impoverishment, for it excluded nothing that it did not itself contain." Murphy finds himself in a padded cell where "the tender luminous oyster-grey of the pneumatic upholstery, cushioning every square inch of ceiling, walls, floor and door, lent colour to the truth, that one was a prisoner of air." Here the setting perfectly captures the paradoxical mood tone of quasi-solipsism, that feeling of being both imprisoned and protected by a pervasive mental atmosphere that inserts itself between reality and the self.[57]

The schizophrenic patient Renée describes the "eerie atmosphere of torpor and mutism," "an all-embracing stupor and indifference," into which she fell and then existed for a long time:

> Everything passed as in a dreary dream; nothing was differentiated, no reaction was possible. Neither the doctors nor the nurses assumed any comprehension of their orders and questions. Yet they were mistaken; I was perfectly aware of what went on, of what was said about me. Indeed, everything had become so totally irrelevant, so devoid of emotion and sensibility that in truth it was the same as though they were not talking to me at all. I simply could not react, the essential motor force had broken down. Images with whom I had nothing to do, from whom I was remote, moved toward and away from my bed. I was, myself, a lifeless image.[58]

Schreber's attitude toward his own physical being seems to have had this dereified and affectless quality, a fact that makes it possible to understand how he could be so calm and matter-of-fact about events which, to the reader, seem fantastic, contradictory, or horrifying. For example, like many schizophrenic patients,[59] Schreber would claim that his body was undergoing all sorts of serious injuries and radical transformations: internal organs "were torn or vanished repeatedly" (M, 134); for long periods of time he lived without a stomach, intestines, or bladder. He believed that he had consumed his own larynx with his food and had eaten up his pharynx several times (M, 272, 135). Yet much of the time he was strangely unworried by these seemingly drastic events and found nothing unusual in the fact that an organ that had been destroyed might reappear after a time, perfectly intact: "I existed frequently without a stomach; I expressly told the attendant M., as he may remember, that I could not eat because I had no stomach. Sometimes immediately before meals a stomach was so to speak produced *ad hoc* by miracles" (M, 133–34). "The inner table of my skull was lined with a different brain membrane in order to extinguish my memory of my own ego"; but, as Schreber says, "all this without any permanent effect" (M, 99). His beliefs about external events or other people were no less bizarre or phantasmagoric. He stated, for instance, that people would sometimes exchange heads with each other, also that certain people, such as his wife and his doctor, were dead; yet most of the time he was not at all surprised, or particularly relieved, to see these people walking about once again among the living.[60]

Schreber does not speculate about objective or physicalistic explanations for such fantastic events. He seems to have experienced such events as occurring in a realm distinct from the natural or actual world, with its constraints and its consequentiality. And this special realm was, apparently, purely experiential—an "ideological domain" where "miracling up" was implicitly felt to involve not amazing physical or biological processes but something more like mental feats, acts of imagination. This, I believe, is what is described by one schizophrenic of the hebephrenic subtype (patients who manifest disorganized speech, incongruous affect, and odd mannerisms), a patient of Eugen Bleuler's who wrote that "the forms are nothing but the above-mentioned personalities (doctors etc. etc.); and they must cease being in the same way in which they originated."[61] As Bleuler explains, the patient meant that the "forms" would cease (the aspects in seeing-as?) but not the real people who were identified with these forms. The delusional world of many schizophrenic-type patients is not, then, a flesh-and-blood world of shared action and risk but a mind's-eye world where emotions, other people, even the patient's own body exist as distant or purely subjective phenomena, mere figments of an abstract imagination whose power is at the same time limitless and irrelevant.[62]

One intriguing passage in the *Memoirs* expresses Schreber's awareness (albeit a somewhat confused and confusing awareness) of this peculiar combination of omnipotence and impotence. He is referring to the fact that, in dealing with "nuisances" such as the persistent voices he heard coming from animals or things, he would feel inclined simply to express his wish that the nuisance would cease—

to say, for example, "If only the cursed railways would cease to speak." On the one hand, Schreber expresses a sense of his own power when he writes, "By willing I can keep out, if only temporarily, all vibrations from outside. Thus, 'I am master of all noises' as the expression goes." But another passage on the same page expresses something very different, the practical man's sense of the impotence of mere wishing:

> Such sentences of course made no practical difference whatever. Indeed the idea that one could stop a nuisance by simply expressing *in words* the wish for it to stop, seems to have been one of the peculiarities of the soul-character. For example: when miracles make my face hot or my feet cold, I am continually urged to *say* aloud: "If only the cursed heat would cease" or "If only my feet weren't so cold"; whereas as a practical human being I naturally prefer to wash my face with cold water instead or to warm my feet by rubbing them. (M. 183)

As we have discussed, the pervasive subjectivization experienced by schizophrenic patients can sometimes keep them from acting in the shared and actual world, perhaps because real action feels irrelevant to them. At other times, however, the delusional experiences of schizophrenics do have consequences for their real-world behavior. This was true even of Schreber: he did, after all, sit still in the garden in order to comply with God's demands and to make the wasp miracle occur; he did pose before the mirror with feminine adornments, as he himself notes. But when such an intermingling of the imaginary with actuality occurs, we should not necessarily assume what the poor reality-testing formula implies—namely, that both realms are taken as real. As we have seen (recall Schreber's experience of his railway trip), it may be that both the delusional and the actual world are felt to be somehow unreal—which can sometimes result in a tendency to confuse the two worlds.[63] *Both* realms may be pervaded by a certain subjectivization or cerebralization, by a cushioning, dereifying process, Beckett's "tender, luminous oyster-grey . . . pneumatic upholstery." And this, perhaps, is what is meant by the following statements from three different schizophrenics:

> For me the substance has become spirit.
>
> The sum total of the spirit is constant, and the crazy thing about it is that it adds up to zero.
>
> Reality, as it was formerly, no longer exists. Real life has suffered a decline.[64]

Only through imagining this kind of lived-world can one begin to understand how schizophrenics could be capable of performing certain real-world actions that, to the normal person, would be unimaginably horrible. In extreme cases, such patients may seriously mutilate themselves—even, for example, cutting off their own genitals or putting out their eyes. Though their sensory organs still function and they are cognitively aware of their actions, they do not appear to experience any pain or to register the significance and irreversibility of what they have done. When one talks to these patients, it almost seems that, for them, everything involved in the action—the body part, the cutting, even the pain itself—is a purely theoretical phenomenon, as if the action had been but a thought experiment, a removal of idea-of-penis or idea-of-eye rather than the actual organ of flesh, blood, and screaming nerve. Many schizophrenic patients often do feel separated from the lived-body: "Body and soul don't belong together; there's no unity," stated one of Manfred Bleuler's patients.[65] And it may be this separation, rather than the polymorphous infantile sexuality postulated by psychoanalysts, that accounts for the uncertain sexual identity in so many of them. One might even understand the tendency for acts of self-mutilation to focus on the genitals in this way—as representing the patient's attempt to bring his idea-of-body into closer correspondence with the purely cerebral nature of his lived world.[66]

THE MORBID DREAMER

Traditional psychiatric and psychoanalytic interpretations often emphasize change in the *content* of experience as the essential motivation for the development of the delusional world. Supposedly, the patient withdraws from a reality experienced as a "malevolent, destructive, unpredictable, chaotic external world" into the "comfort and solace" of an "unrealistic fantasy world" of benevolent objects and "blissful satisfaction"—thus denying the reality of an unwanted state of affairs in order to replace it with one more satisfying or more flattering.[67] According to this classic view, the delusional world is in fact unreal, but the patient experiences it (or at least wants to experience it) as real. The quasi-solipsist interpretation turns on its head this psychoanalytic view, arguing that the delusional world is preferred not in spite of but because of its felt unreality. Jean-Paul Sartre presents such an alternative view in *The Psychology of Imagination*. He describes the delusions (they might better be termed so-called delusions, in Schreber's phrase) of what he calls the "morbid dreamer" as involving an attempt to escape not so much the content as the form of the real—its ultimate, frightening unknowability and its tendency both to demand and to resist real-world action.[68] By focusing on the subjectivized quality of an unreal world, a world constituted by oneself, the patient manages to escape the anxieties inherent in experiencing the limits of one's actual knowledge and power. A schizophrenic patient quoted by Manfred Bleuler sums up this aspect of the delusional world nicely: "In my world I am omnipotent; in yours I practice diplomacy."[69]

Despite its devitalization and isolation, this solipsistic realm might almost be serene—were it not for a peculiar sense of responsibility and an attendant anxiety that creep in to fill the vacuum left by the departure of normal sources of fear, sadness, pain, and passion. The anxiety of this quasi-solipsistic universe is ontological and totalistic, however. It occupies itself not with this or that concern *within* the framework of the real (Will I succeed? Am I loved?) but with something more bloodless and abstract, the sense of the flimsiness of a universe that depends for its existence on a constituting consciousness. "Everything seems to slip away into impressions. . . . For what is, is, and yet what seems to be is always changing and drifting away into thought and ideas, rather than actualities," said the schizoaffective patient quoted earlier in this chapter. What is threatening about such experiences concerns the ontological framework itself.[70]

As abstract, cerebral, and even theoretical as such anxieties may sound, they can be intense, immediate, and experientially very real.

Unlike the skeptical philosopher who can leave his metaphysical speculations behind in his study, many schizophrenics live the solipsistic vision with a certain literalness, which may express itself in a feeling that combines ultimate responsiblity with awesome fear. "The whole world turned in my head. I was the axis," was one schizophrenic's way of expressing his centrality in the universe.[71] But such a sense of immeasurable power can also turn against the patient, resulting in the most profound of all schizophrenic fears—the delusions of world catastrophe. One catatonic patient explained why she would hold herself immobile for hours in an uncomfortable position, her arm upraised and standing on her toes; it was, she said, for the purpose of "stopping the world march to catastrophe": "If I succeed in remaining in a perfect state of suspension, I will suspend the movement of the earth and stop the march of the world to destruction."[72] The prisoner of her own unimaginable power, she seems to have been afraid to give up the solipsistic stance of rigid and passive hyperconcentration for fear of upsetting the cosmos.[73]

It seems clear, in any case, that the solipsistic stance, no matter how rigidly maintained, can never provide the haven of absolute safety for which the patient yearns. In the pages to follow, we shall see how fraught with internal contradictions solipsism really is, and how inevitably it undermines its own sources of security and power.

2

ENSLAVED SOVEREIGN, OBSERVED SPECTATOR

Man appears in his ambiguous position as an object of knowledge and as a subject that knows: enslaved sovereign, observed spectator.

—Michel Foucault, *The Order of Things*

The solipsistic interpretation of schizophrenic experience can certainly account for many aspects of delusions that seem to be inconsistent with the traditional poor reality-testing formula. To some readers, however—especially those who have had considerable personal contact with schizophrenic individuals—this interpretation may seem a bit too neat. They may be troubled by the existence of certain characteristics of such persons that I have neglected, characteristics that appear to undermine a solipsistic reading.

It cannot be denied that such patients do at times make claims that give every appearance of being delusional in the traditional sense, claims that refer to an external or consensual reality beyond the confines of a purely subjective realm and that could legitimately be said to be falsifiable in objective or consensual terms. Also, such patients often enough have experiences that appear directly to contradict the essential solipsistic experience of being the center of the universe and the only conscious being. Rather than feeling their own consciousness to be the constituting foundation of the All, they often experience their actions or thoughts as under the scrutiny and control, or in the presence or possession, of some alien and presumably more encompassing other mind—as is the case with several of

Schneider's first-rank symptoms of schizophrenia. Schreber, for example, frequently felt himself to be the object of attention of God or of the rays, which he knew to be the nerves of God; and, strangely enough, his very feeling of being the center of the universe often coincided with a feeling of being in the presence of another consciousness, that of God (M, 60, 215). This is apparent in one passage which was partially quoted in Chapter 1: "I had to assume and was forced by my experiences to assume, that if God were permanently tied to my person, all creation on earth would have to perish with the exception of some play-with-miracles in my immediate surroundings" (M, 60). Finally, some schizophrenics even come to feel that, far from being omnipotent, their own consciousness does not exist at all: "I am not alive, I cannot move," said one patient; "I have no mind, and no feelings; I have never existed, people only thought I did."[1]

In this chapter, I treat such aspects of Schreber's lived-world, first by considering whether and how his solipsistic claims might be intended to have implications regarding objective or consensual reality, then by considering the nature of the self—the "I-experience" or lack thereof—implicit in his solipsistic world. Such features of the schizophrenic world are not only problematic for the solipsistic reading I am offering; they imply that there is something inadequate and even misleading about certain basic linguistic and conceptual distinctions on which we usually depend, to understand as well as to describe. For it seems that, in such a world, everything can be both "real" and "unreal," both "inner" and "outer," both "subjective" and "objective." But how are we to grasp this impossible universe, where everything is felt to belong to the self, yet where there may be no self to possess it?

Once again, Wittgenstein has preceded us in considering the same paradoxes that we find at the core of the schizophrenic's seemingly incomprehensible form of life. To demonstrate the illogicality of solipsism, he offers a series of arguments, and each of these corresponds rather closely to the existential anomalies at issue. With each anomaly, much of what at first seems inconsistent with the solipsistic reading turns out, on closer analysis, to be an intrinsic and inevitable element of the inherently paradoxical stance of solipsism itself.

EQUIVOCATION BETWEEN THE SUBJECTIVE AND THE OBJECTIVE

Given the solipsistic interpretation of the delusional world, one might expect a patient like Schreber to restrict himself to assertions about the realm of the subjective, the purely experiential reality that looms up before him alone. One might expect him to behave like a phenomenologist who brackets external reality by refraining from assertions about any thing-in-itself independent of his own mind. One might also expect a solipsistic patient to refrain from proselytizing. For, if his is a subjective vision, and felt as such, how could he possibly expect others to grasp it? How, in fact, could there even *be* others—others with consciousness—given the revelation of the absolute epistemic centrality and uniqueness of his own isolated and constituting self?[2]

At times, Schreber does behave in this internally consistent or expected fashion. Indeed, in the following passage he sounds almost like a phenomenological investigator bracketing the question of the real: "As before when discussing supernatural matters [which corresponds to the realm of his delusional experiences and beliefs], I have to confine myself to relating impressions which I received and can only conjecture in how far these changes were objective events. I recollect that for a longish period there appeared to be a *smaller* sun" (M, 124). After describing a bizarre experience of hearing voices exclaiming that he had "a plurality of heads," Schreber writes, "I am fully aware how fantastic all this must sound to other people; and I therefore do not go so far as to assert that all I have recounted was objective reality; I only relate the impressions retained as recollections in my memory" (M, 86).[3] Further, he states in several passages that he has no intention of proselytizing concerning his belief in miracles and other supernatural phenomena because his "Kingdom" is not of this world but rather something seen in the mind's eye. Also, his certainty is of a degree and a kind that makes it, as he says, "completely immaterial to me what other people think of the truth or probability of my ideas" (M, 186, 301–2). He explains that a full understanding would be impossible for others since they have not had the same experiences as he himself; and he states, "Things are dealt with which cannot be expressed in human language; they exceed human understanding" (M, 41). At such times, Schreber seems to display an almost Wittgensteinian appreciation of the utter privacy and ineffability of the solipsistic vision, its status as a mere assertion or as a sort of mood that cannot be justified in any logical or public fashion.[4]

But at other times Schreber takes a different line, as if he were being irresistibly drawn out of his private space toward a consensual and objective world. When he begins his memoirs with the statement "I have come infinitely closer to the truth than human beings who have not received divine revelation" (M, 41), it certainly sounds as if he were planning to make assertions about an objective truth that others might be brought to accept. And, as we saw above, when he saw the sun fill a large part of the sky, he initially expected the attendant M to share this vision. Also, Schreber wanted to convince others that, in the wasp miracle, insects really did come into being around him and not elsewhere. Regarding this and other instances of the "divine miracle" of "spontaneous generation," he states, "My aim is to show the reader that he is not only dealing with the empty figments of a poor mental patient's fantasy" (M, 183–86). And in other passages he writes, "The Director of the Asylum can hardly doubt that with these expositions I am pursuing not only my personal interests but also those of science." "I believe I have thus furnished proof which must arouse serious doubt among serious men as to whether what has so far been attributed to hallucinations and delusions is not after all reality, and therefore my whole belief in their miraculous nature and my explanation of the phenomena on my person and on my body not also founded on truth" (M, 206, 207).

In the *Memoirs*, Schreber discusses the nature of God and the Beyond and of "the Order of the World"; he describes an elaborate cosmos of nerves, rays, and spirits which, presumably, could be acknowledged by his readers also. Indeed, the very purpose of writing his memoirs was "to further knowledge of truth in a vital field, that of religion," by telling others about "experiences which—when generally acknowledged as valid—will act fruitfully to the highest possible degree among the rest of mankind" (M, 33, also 155n). "The time will come," he writes, "when other human beings will also have to recognize as a fact that my person has become the center of divine miracles" (M, 192). Further, "It need hardly be said what incalculable gain it would be for mankind if, through my personal fate, . . . the foundations of mere materialism and of hazy pantheism would once and for all be abolished" (M, 79).

Schreber's claims seem, then, to involve a contradiction—or at least a continual equivocation—between two attitudes: one in which he accepts the essential innerness and privacy of his own claims, the other in which he assumes that they have some kind of objectivity and potential consensuality. This duality is hardly unique to Schreber: many schizophrenic patients who seem generally aware of the innerness of their claims also consider their delusions to be revelations of a truth that they assume to be, in some sense, both objective and potentially public in nature.[5] On its face, this certainly appears to contradict my interpretation: the tendency to claim a kind of truth value for delusions seems consistent with the poor reality-testing formula I have criticized; and shifting between a solipsistic vision and a kind of poor reality-testing might suggest the tolerance for contradiction so characteristic of primitive primary-process modes of thought. Wittgenstein's meditations can, however, offer another way of viewing many such deviations or equivocations of the solipsistic mode—one that explains them not as contradictions of solipsism but as a playing out of the inherently self-refuting nature of solipsism itself.[6]

Wittgenstein shows that a solipsist must inevitably equivocate between two ways of claiming the world as his own. He points out that if the solipsist referred with absolute consistency and self-insight only to the experienced world—the "visual room" or "visual stove" are Wittgenstein's examples—such a person would have to recognize the emptiness of his claim that "the world is my world." For to say that the room-as-seen-by-me can only be seen by me is tautologous; it is what Wittgenstein calls a merely grammatical move. It is only because we imagine the "visual room" as somehow analogous to an actual room that such a statement seems meaningful and even profound. Only because we imagine (mistakenly) that things might have been different—that the "visual room," that is, *my* visual room, might, like a physical room, *not* have belonged to me—is the tautology able to masquerade as a statement. In Wittgenstein's words:

> "At any rate only I have got THIS."—What are these words for? They serve no purpose.—Can one not add: "There is here no question of a 'seeing'—and therefore none of a 'having'—nor of a subject, nor therefore of 'I' either"? Might I not ask: In what sense have you *got* what you are talking about and saying that only you have got it? Do you possess it? . . . And this too is clear: If as a matter of logic you exclude other people's having something, it loses its sense to say that you have it. (PI, §398)

Elsewhere he writes, "If the Solipsist says he has something which another hasn't, he is absurd" (L, 15–16).

Wittgenstein pursues this point by considering what he calls the grammar of such words as "here," "I," and "this"—words that are absolutely central to the vision of the solipsist since without them he cannot express his dubious claims (PI, §410). Such words, known in linguistics as indexicals or shifters, tend to be thought of as analogous to proper names, though in fact they are quite different. Thus, the solipsist who mouths the tautologies "this room is *my* room" or "the center of the universe is *here*" believes he is making an empirical statement on the order of "the dining room is my room" or "the center of the universe is at Hollywood and Vine." But "here" is not like "Hollywood and Vine," since the referent of "here" has no independent anchoring and shifts with the speaker. In using such an indexical, the solipsist only *seems* to be making an assertion. His statement is in fact empty, a mere statement that "here is here." The solipsist—to borrow one of Wittgenstein's many metaphors for the futility of such metaphysical claims—is like someone who tries to measure his own height not by using an independent reference system but by placing his own hand on top of his head.

Schreber makes precisely this error, and it is an important source of his paranoid-grandiose sense that, as he puts it, "everything that happens is in reference to me" (M, 197).[7] Thus, he feels he has *discovered* a surprising empirical fact, that experience happens only here, when in fact *his* experience could not on principle happen anywhere else anyway. Rather portentously, Schreber writes, "It is by no means impossible that seeing [*Sehvermögen*] . . . is confined to my person and immediate surroundings" (M, 232). "I can no longer doubt that the so-called 'play with human beings' (the effect of miracles) is limited to myself and *to whatever constitutes my immediate environment at the time*" (M, 32).[8] His proof of this "discovery" is curiously circular, in just the tautologous way Wittgenstein describes. This can be seen in the following passage, in which Schreber seems to be arguing, in essence, that the proof that miracles only happen here is that they only happen here:

> In any case miracles occur only on my person or in my immediate vicinity. I have again received striking proof of this in the last few days which I think is worth mentioning here. . . . The following afternoon several gambolling mosquitos were similarly produced by miracle in front of my face while I sat in the garden of the inn of the neighbouring village of Ebenheit during an excursion; and again they appeared *only* in my immediate vicinity. (M, 233)[9]

We have seen that experiential events like the wasp miracle are essentially moments when Schreber feels a welling up of the solipsistic feeling that "this wasp is *my* wasp" (that is, that the wasp appears only to *me*). So it is hardly surprising that *such* experiences only happen here; it is, after all, not a contingent but a necessary feature of them to happen here. Notice the equivocation inherent in Schreber's phrase "my immediate vicinity": although he may think he is referring to the kind of place that could be objectively defined ("by the bench," for example, as opposed to "over by the wall of the garden"), in actuality "my immediate vicinity" means something more like "wherever I happen to look."

Because Schreber, not unlike solipsists in the history of philosophy, fails to recognize this fact, what is really an utter banality ("here is here") hits him with all the force of revelation. He feels he has discovered something substantial and remarkable when, in fact, he has simply adopted a certain attitude toward experience and an associated manner of speaking—what Wittgenstein calls, respectively, a "new way of looking at things" and "a grammatical move." Wittgenstein's analysis of a common form of philosophical error seems, then, to be precisely on the mark. Simply substitute "visual wasp" for "visual room" in the following passage from the *Philosophical Investigations*, and you have a description and deconstruction of Schreber's "miracled-up" world:

> The 'visual room' seemed like a discovery, but what its discoverer really found was a new way of speaking, a new comparison; it might even be called a new sensation.
>
> You have a new conception and interpret it as seeing a new object. You interpret a grammatical movement made by yourself as a quasi-physical phenomenon which you are observing. (Think for example of the question: "Are sense-data the material of which the universe is made?")
>
> But there is an objection to my saying that you have made a 'grammatical' movement. What you have primarily discovered is a new way of looking at things. As if you had invented a new way of painting; or, again, a new metre, or a new kind of song. (PI, §§400–401)

One implication of Wittgenstein's analysis is that to feel the solipsistic vision as revelation is necessarily to have the urge to go beyond a strictly consistent solipsism. Solipsism only feels powerful, worth taking seriously, if one smuggles in, by a legerdemain invisible even to oneself, the conceptual framework of the *normal* form of life—the realm where it makes some sense to speak of (objective) rooms belonging to a person. Equivocation between solipsism and what one might call the natural attitude turns out to be endemic to quasi-solipsism. It follows that we should not be surprised to find Schreber wavering between a purely subjective sense of revelation and one that seems to contain implications concerning the consensual and objective world.

To realize the truth of what Wittgenstein says is to dissolve the sense of revelation inherent in the solipsistic vision. But Wittgenstein's analysis also shows that the solipsist who feels the sense of his own centrality as revelation is necessarily caught up in a self-contradictory attempt to move beyond this centrality—by trying to communicate his solipsistic insight as if it were relevant to other consciousnesses and by claiming a paradoxical ownership of a world whose status equivocates oddly between the objective and the subjective. Thus the solipsist is driven to want what he can never have, validation in the consensual world, and this undercuts his seeming self-sufficiency. Such validation is doubly impossible, for on principle others cannot acknowledge the revelation; and even if they could, their very acknowledging would contradict the essence of the revelation itself.

As we have seen, however, the solipsist is nevertheless driven to communicate and to convince. Schreber, for example, writes of wanting to demolish "mere materialism" and "hazy pantheism" to make way in our minds for the true Order of the World (M, 79)—an ambition that, we must presume, means making public the truth of his own (private) solipsistic vision. With its peculiar combination of doubt and certitude, of diffidence and proselytizing zeal, Schreber's *Memoirs* manifests the paradoxical yearning that is central to the delusional world of madness. Indeed, the very act of writing the *Memoirs*—which, as Schreber tells us in his introduction, is intended to communicate with and to convince his readers—testifies to the fundamental contradiction and the potential sources of vulnerability that can lie at the heart of an autistic world.[10]

SELF AS ALL, SELF AS NOTHING: SCHREBER'S EXPERIENCE

I turn now to a second feature of Schreber's lived-world which seems in conflict with my solipsistic interpretation, one that takes us to the heart of his perplexing experience of self. It is often assumed that the central insight of solipsism is the idea that the self is the center or owner of those experiences that are declared to be all there is. In the words of the philosopher P. M. S. Hacker, "solipsism is the doctrine according to which nothing exists save myself and mental states of myself."[11] One thing implied here is a certain subjectivization of the lived-world—a quality which, as we have seen, Schreber's world does possess. But there is also another implication: that the solipsist *has* an experiencing self—and it is not always clear that Schreber does feel this.

Some readers may already have noted a strange suggestion in Schreber's way of speaking, the occasional implication that he feels or believes that the subjectivized world he experiences does not belong to Schreber himself. When he says "I am represented as a woman," for example, there seems an implication that the representing that construes him as (sees him as) female belongs either to some other being or conscious center or to no one at all. At one point, Schreber explicitly describes two forms of subjectivization—he calls them miracles—which differ according to who carries out the picturing or representing. In one case, picturing feels like an act of the self. Schreber refers to this as a "reversed miracle": "In the same way as rays throw onto my nerves pictures they would like to see especially in dreams, I too can in turn produce pictures for the rays which I want them to see" (M, 181). But in the other (apparently standard) case of miracles, picturing takes place at a remove, as an act performed by God, by "one," or by rays, which manipulate his nerve medium for their own purposes. These latter instances involve a strange combination of subjectivization and externality that seems inconsistent with solipsism. Though the feminization, or other picturing, is somehow felt to take place in *the* mind's eye, it apparently is not felt to occur in *my* mind's eye.

This double suggestion comes across distinctly in the following two passages, which are quoted at length and demand a careful reading. In them we find the most overt general statements in the *Memoirs* of Schreber's solipsistic realization, expressed in the idea that "seeing," or consciousness, is confined to Schreber's own immediate vicinity. But they also contain his apparently contradictory speculation that what seems to be his experience may really belong to some other being—namely, God or "one" (the latter being so nonspecific as to amount, perhaps, to no particular being at all). The uncanny and logically impossible qualities so characteristic of the schizophrenic world are evident in these passages. In reading them, one approaches that heart of darkness, the very core of schizophrenic incomprehensibility:

> Since God entered into exclusive nerve-contact with me, and I thus became the sole human being on whom his interest centers, the highly important question arises, whether His capacity to see and hear is confined to my person and to what happens around me. I dare not answer this question yet; but the experiences of the future will most probably afford me reliable indication for a positive or negative answer to this question. It is unquestionable that the light and heat emanating from the sun is spread now, as before, over the whole earth; but it is by no means impossible that seeing, which is a faculty of the rays (that is of the totality of God's nerves) is confined to my person and immediate surroundings—like one used to say for many years after the 1870 war about the foreign policy of the French, that they stared at the gap in the Vosges as if hypno-

tized. . . . In any case miracles occur only on my person or in my immediate vicinity. (M, 232–33)

I can put this point briefly: *everything that happens is in reference to me.* . . . Since God entered into nerve contact with me exclusively, I became in a way for God the only human being, or simply the human being around whom everything turns, to whom everything that happens must be related and who therefore, from his own point of view, must also relate all things to himself.

This completely absurd conception, which was at first naturally incomprehensible to me but which I was forced to acknowledge as a fact through years of experience, becomes apparent at every opportunity and occasion. For instance, when I read a book or a newspaper, one thinks that the ideas in them are my own; when I play a song or an opera arrangement for the piano, one thinks that the text of the song or opera expresses my own feelings. (M, 197)[12]

It is common for Schreber to speak of "one" who wished or perceived a given phenomenon, or to use the passive voice to describe his own thoughts, perceptions, or feelings. His translators warn that expressions like "one felt that I" or "it was said that I" indicate some basic confusion about himself on Schreber's part and are not to be dismissed as slapdash translations (M, 27). In such manners of expression, there does seem to be a double and paradoxical suggestion. In the second of the passages just quoted, for example, there is both the implication that Schreber's own experiences are all that exists (i.e., all ideas and feelings are his own) as well as the implication that his experiences do not in some crucial way really belong to him—since it is some other being, "one," who has the *awareness* that these are Schreber's experiences. In other passages, usually in the passive voice (for example, "I am represented as a woman"), the experiences are not ascribed to anyone at all, not even to "one," that vaguest of beings.

It seems that, on the one hand, Schreber feels himself to be the conscious center of the universe, the owner and origin of all experience; on the other hand, what would certainly be expected to *be* his own experience, the very feeling of owning his sensations, feelings, and ideas, is itself felt to belong to "one" rather than to Schreber himself or else not to belong to anyone at all. Also worth noting is the hint of tautology in a line from the second passage quoted above, concerning the person who, "*from his own point of view* [*von seinem Standpunkte*], must also relate all things to himself" (emphasis added). Schreber's phrasing suggests at least an implicit awareness that the sense of centrality is relevant only to himself and not to the objective or consensual world—as if he experiences, perhaps even recognizes, the circular or tautological aspect of his solipsistic position.[13]

A similar disowning or depersonalization is characteristic of Schreber's auditory hallucinations or quasi-hallucinations (as is the case with many psychotic patients in the schizophrenia spectrum). In such experiences, it is usually obvious that what Schreber is hearing are his own thoughts as if they were spoken aloud. But not only does he hear these thoughts as if they were spoken by external voices; these voices often use a curiously impersonal and detached idiom that implies that the thought is neither controlled nor even possessed by any identifiable being: for example, "it was said that I"; "it is hoped that voluptuousness has reached a certain degree" (M, 27, 236).[14] It is not uncommon for schizoid and schizophenic persons to drop the first person as subject or doer in favor of a more impersonal language ("the thought occurred that").[15]

The coexistence of quasi-solipsism and loss of the sense of controlling or owning one's own action and experience is especially clear in a passage from the *Memoirs* quoted earlier: "Whenever a butterfly appears my gaze is *first* directed to it as to a being newly created that very moment, and *secondly* the words 'butterfly—has been recorded' are spoken into my nerves by the voices; this shows that one thought I could possibly no longer recognize a butterfly and one therefore examines me to find out whether I still know the meaning of the word 'butterfly'" (M, 188).[16] Here Schreber appears to sense that the world of objects depends on him (the newly created or "miracled-up" butterfly exists only for him) while simultaneously feeling his own consciousness to be a pawn and an object of scrutiny of some other mind—namely, the "one" who directs his gaze and examines him to find out whether he still knows the meaning of the word "butterfly." Like many schizophrenic patients, Schreber combines a sense of omnipotence with a sense of abject subjugation and powerlessness. His own consciousness plays two seemingly incompatible roles: for he experiences his own mind as the hub around which the universe revolves, the indispensible constitutor on which it depends, as if he were a sort of unmoved prime mover, but he also feels his own experience to be limited and constrained, like something contemplated and manipulated (perhaps even constituted) by some distant and ever-receding other mind. Thus "seeing," the source of Being, happens only "here," and Schreber's whims control the weather (though only in the mind's eye; M, 181); yet Schreber is also totally enslaved, not only under the constant scrutiny of "one," but with his gaze being directed without his will toward those very insects that exist only for him.

A similar equivocation is reflected in Schreber's odd relationship to God, perhaps the central preoccupation of the *Memoirs*. On the one hand, Schreber feels intimate with God and God's awareness: "God is inseparably tied to my person through my nerves' power of attraction which for some time past has become inescapable; there is no possibility of God freeing Himself from my nerves for the rest of my life" (M, 209). Also relevant is Schreber's description, in the first of the two long passages quoted above, of the confinement of God's "seeing" to Schreber's own immediate vicinity. Schreber compares God's confinement to a passive fascination: it is, he says, like the French staring "at the gap in the Vosges as if hypnotized" (thereby failing to notice what lies beyond their focus of attention). Here God's attitude or mode of consciousness seems strikingly similar to Schreber's own: God, like Schreber himself, adopts, or is caught up in, a stance of passive hyperconcentration—the very attitude that is likely, on Wittgenstein's account, to underlie the solipsistic experience of constituting the world. For both God and Schreber, awareness is felt to be restricted, yet this restriction is associated with the feeling of being a quasi-divine consciousness. In Schreber's vision, God is generally equated with awareness, an awareness that vivifies and grounds the world. It is also true that all God's awareness, all he knows, comes through Schreber himself—who, Schreber says, is the only conscious human being and the conduit by which God can know: "Seeing, which is a faculty of the rays (that is of the totality of God's nerves) is confined to my person and immediate surroundings." The implications seem inescapable: not only must

God himself be a solipsist; Schreber and God are, in some sense, one and the same being.

The fact remains, however, that Schreber also experiences God as alien—indeed, as a being who stands for the very essence of pure Otherness. Schreber calls him "the *distant* God" and reports that God's divine representatives call him "I Who am distant [*Entfernten, der ich bin*]." God is the one who "retire[s] to an enormous distance," a place from which, however, he continues to monitor Schreber's experience (M, 160n, 191). Since this is the same God who, Schreber feels, looks out at the world through Schreber's own eyes, one can only conclude that Schreber experiences his own perceptions as belonging, at least at times, not to himself but to some separate and distant being. His notion of God, the "I Who am distant," captures this curious contradiction, this sense of both being and not being the epistemic, constituting center of the universe. Incidentally, if one bears in mind Schreber's close identification of God's consciousness with his own, adding to this his tendency to experience the world itself as a manifestation of God's consciousness—"I dare not decide whether one can simply say that God and the heavenly bodies are one and the same. . . . one can speak figuratively of the sun and light of the stars as the eye of God" (M, 46–47)—one grasps an even more extreme implication: the possibility that Schreber sometimes experiences the whole world not just as depending on but as *manifesting* his own being, as if the All were made out of Schreber-substance.

In the *Memoirs*, God's contradictory qualities are sometimes expressed, and in some fashion accommodated, through the use of traditional theological concepts or ways of speaking, as when Schreber warns that the God he experiences ought not to be thought of as "limited in space by the confines of a body like a human being, but one has to think of him as Many in One or One in Many" (M, 160n). Nevertheless, Schreber is often troubled by the apparent contradictoriness as well as the possible blasphemy inherent in his claims about his own centrality and his special relationship to God. He wonders, for example, how God could *be* God, the all-powerful, all-knowing one, and the creator of all humans, if indeed he depends so fully, for the knowledge he has, on a human being such as Schreber (M, 220–21). But elsewhere he writes that "one Schreber soul more or less" did not seem to matter to the existence of the realms of God since "one felt so possessed of immense power that the possibility of one single human being ever becoming a danger to God Himself was not taken into consideration" (M, 58). Still, Schreber cannot help but question God's overweaning confidence: God's existence *does* seem to be so bound up with Schreber's own that Schreber has to ask himself, "What is to become of God—if I may so express myself—should I die?" (M, 213).

Esoteric and tortured as this discussion may sound, it concerns a very real and central feature of the experience of many schizophrenic patients. One of the most characteristic features of this enigmatic and uneasy form of existence is a strange equivocation or oscillation between what would seem to be antithetical feelings—a sense of absolute centrality and omniscience, of boundless power and importance, on the one hand, and, on the other, feelings of infinite smallness, weakness, or unimportance bordering on nonexistence. "I feel nameless, impersonal," said one patient, "my gaze is fixed like a corpse; my mind has become vague and general; like a nothing or the absolute."[17]

This oscillation can also be expressed in spatial or substantial terms. Schreber senses at times that his boundaries extend to the ends of the universe: "It appeared that nerves—probably taken from my body—were strung over the whole heavenly vault" (M, 109). But he also feels that he is tiny, an almost nonexistent being lost in the vastness of space. One of Herbert Rosenfeld's patients experienced herself as waxing and waning—at times swelling up like a balloon to many times her normal size, at other moments shrinking to a tiny point at the center of the vast balloon.[18] The poet and man of the theater Antonin Artaud, who was schizophrenic, expressed a related experience in more abstract terms. To some ears, his words may seem cryptic, a manifestation of that poverty of content supposedly characteristic of schizophrenic discourse. But those who return to the following quotation after finishing this chapter may feel that Artaud is actually giving a quite literal and precise description of the true nature of this essentially epistemological oscillation: "Like life, like nature, thought goes from the inside out before going from the outside in. I begin to think in the void and from the void I move toward the plenum; and when I have reached the plenum I can fall back into the void. I go from the abstract to the concrete and not from the concrete toward the abstract."[19]

Paradoxical though it may seem, these two experiences—self as all, self as nothing—can even coexist at the same moment. During a catatonic period, a patient of mine had the experience of taking off his own head and walking down the vast tunnel of his trachea, where he moved about while examining a new universe composed of his own internal organs. Thus, he himself was simultaneously both the vast surrounding universe and the observing being dwarfed by this universe. Further, the world took on a strangely insubstantial quality during this experience, a quality of unreality suggestive of subjectivization. It was, he said, as if everything were composed not of real things but of transparencies like those used in architect's drawings.

Another aspect of the paradoxical sense of self is suggested by this same patient, who, after saying that the world seemed like a set of transparent blueprints or copies, described feeling himself to be the Xerox machine that produced these copies. The image suggests that he experienced himself as a paradoxical being—a sort of consciousness machine, devoid of volitional control but nevertheless capable of creating and constituting the universe. The paradox here recalls Schreber's feeling of being watched as his gaze moved (as if out of his own control) toward the "miracled-up" butterfly. Such a lived-world might be described as involving a sort of solipsistic tunnel vision: the patient experiences his own consciousness as constituting the very world itself while also experiencing it as an empirical fact *in* the world, as a channel of limited capacity and an object of possible observation and control (the Xerox machine). He is, as it were, caught in a tunnel of light, which both feels and does not feel like the sum total of the All.[20]

In their various ways, such experiences reflect a loss or diminishment of self, and this seems to contradict the subjectivization I have been emphasizing. Such a loss or attenuation of selfhood is, however, as common in schizophrenia as is the subjectivization. Indeed, in many cases the two experiences even coexist simultaneously. But how can this be? How can the self be both everything and nonexistent? How, in the same patient and even at the same moment, can the self serve as the all-powerful foundation of the universe while also existing as a fact in the world? Are we confronted here with an instance of sheer incomprehensibility, or is it possible to make some sense of this seeming combination? Once again, Wittgenstein's treatment of solipsism is of help. By following his analysis, we can see this strange loss of self for what it is: an intrinsic and even predictable outgrowth of the peculiar inner logic of solipsism itself.[21]

SELF AS ALL, SELF AS NOTHING: WITTGENSTEIN'S ANALYSIS

According to Wittgenstein, the solipsistic position harbors within itself a tendency toward self-contradiction, toward undermining what at first appears to be its own most fundamental premise. The solipsist begins by believing that the profound realness of his own experience testifies to the centrality of his role in the universe: "When anything is seen (really *seen*), it is always I who see it," is Wittgenstein's statement of this realization (BBB, 61). The solipsist seems to point at the vividness of his private world and thereby to draw a conclusion about the privileged and important position of his own self, which, so to speak, owns these experiences and makes them possible. Rigid staring gives me the feeling that only my experience of the present moment is real. The certainty that, "at any rate, only I have got THIS" (PI, §398) leads to the feeling that "I *am* in a favored position, I am the center of the world" (NFL, 299n), or that "I am the vessel of life" (BBB, 65). As Schopenhauer, the inspiration for Wittgenstein's own youthful solipsism, put it, "The whole of nature outside the knowing subject, and so all remaining individuals, [seem to] exist only in his representation; . . . he is conscious of them always only as his representation, and so merely indirectly, and as something dependent on his own inner being and existence."[22]

But, argues Wittgenstein, if the solipsist is honest and faithful to his principles, he will soon recognize a contradiction in this inference. If he closely scrutinizes his experiences—which, according to the solipsist's own claims, are all that exists—he must admit that he does not find himself there. "'Surely,' I want to say, 'if I'm to be quite frank I must say that I have something which nobody has.'—But who's I?" (NFL, 283). An internally consistent solipsism could find the owner of an experience only *within* that experience, but this would not be the kind of epistemic or constituting owner whose existence the solipsist wants to assert. A somewhat difficult passage from Wittgenstein expresses this point: "Think of a picture of a landscape, an imaginary landscape with a house in it.—Someone asks 'Whose house is that?'—The answer, by the way, might be 'It belongs to the farmer who is sitting on the bench in front of it' " (PI, §398). But if one gives such an answer, it follows that the house that is owned cannot be the "visual house," since the farmer does not contain the (visual) experience in question but, rather, dwells within it. The farmer would not own or constitute the "visual house," for he would exist next to it, within the same plane of reality. The implication is that, even if one did see oneself in one's experience, that self, being within the phenomenal field, could exist only as an object, not in the role of all-powerful constituting subjectivity for which the solipsist yearns. "One might also say," Wittgenstein writes, "Surely the owner of the visual room would have to be the same kind of thing as it is; but he is not to be found in it, and there is no outside" (PI, §399).

It seems that, wherever the solipsist looks, he can find only particular experiential objects—visual images, kinesthetic sensations, and the like. Yet these are objects, not signs of the self. Nowhere do they wear, like monograms, identifying marks that refer them back to me as their owner. As Wittgenstein says, "If anybody asks me to describe *what I see*, I describe *what's seen*" (NFL, 308).[23] And nowhere within experience is the self-as-subject, the supposed owner of experience, to be found. It seems, then, that there is no evidence within experience for asserting the important role of one's own self, understood as a unique ego, in grounding the world. To express this, Schopenhauer used an image Wittgenstein would later echo. He compared the "I" to the "dark point in consciousness": "Just as on the retina the precise point of entry of the optic nerve is blind . . . the eye sees everything except itself."[24]

As a result, argues Wittgenstein, the usual and unrigorous form of solipsism ("the world is my world") reduces by its own intrinsic logic to what might be called a "no-ownership solipsism of the present moment"—a position that can be expressed as "whenever anything is seen, it is this which is seen." The undeniable reality of the experience one *has* turns out not to affirm the existence of the self one *is*. Or, as Wittgenstein puts it, "The idea of a person doesn't enter in the description of [the visual field], just as a [physical] eye doesn't enter into a description of what is seen" (L, 13). "For if the *world* is idea, it isn't any person's idea" (NFL, 297). Wittgenstein also insists—contrary to what a philosopher like Husserl might claim—that there is no evidence for any sort of *impersonal*, transcendental ego or center constituting the world, since there is only the world that *is* experienced and no evidence of anything else. The expression "I" can therefore be eliminated in the context of primary experience: what we should say is "it thinks," like "it rains," and not "I think" (L, 13–14).[25]

One might still claim that the self-as-subject exists, but just not in the same *way* that the objects of experience exist—that "the subject is not part of the world but a presupposition of its existence" (Wittgenstein, NB, 79). But for the solipsist who engages in a scrutinizing hyperawareness, insisting on the unreality of all that goes beyond that which is phenomenally present in a direct and almost concrete fashion, such a position would be contradictory. One might as well admit the existence of other minds, for they too can be invoked as presuppositions of observable facts (like facial expressions and sentences that seem to express or imply experiences on the part of the speaker). No, the rigorous, hyperscrutinizing solipsist must not assume the existence of the self but only of that which is directly observed: experiences.

The paradoxical result, as Wittgenstein puts it in a famous line from the *Tractatus Logico-Philosophicus*, is that "solipsism, when its implications are followed out strictly, coincides with pure realism. The self of solipsism shrinks to a point without extension and there remains the reality co-ordinated with it" (§5.64). Subjectivity, pushed to its outer limit, collapses into objectivity—ending in a sort of narcissism without Narcissus. "I am my world," as Wittgenstein succinctly states it (TLP §5.63; NB, 84)—or, as Artaud might have said, we move from the void toward the plenum and then fall back into the void. The schizophrenic experience of swelling up to fill the world, yet of also being infinitesimal, only a negligible point at the center of the vastness, can be understood as the expression of this solipsistic oscillation. Autobiographical accounts like the following, common enough in schizophrenia, seem to describe just such a development, this process whereby a quasi-solipsistic scrutiny of one's own consciousness leads to a loss of the feeling of any perduring or transcendent self capable of owning its experiences:

> I feel my body breaking up into bits. I get all mixed up so that I don't know myself. I feel like more than one person when this happens. I'm falling apart into bits. . . . I'm frightened to say a word in case everything goes fleeing from me so that there's nothing in my mind. It puts me in a trance that's worse than death. There's a kind of hypnotism going on.
>
> My head's full of thoughts, fears, hates, jealousies. My head can't grip them; I can't hold on to them. I'm behind the bridge of my nose—I mean, my consciousness is there. They're splitting open my head, oh, that's schizophrenic, isn't it? I don't know whether I have these thoughts or not.[26]

The argument I have been considering is a phenomenological one: I have traced out, primarily in the perceptual sphere, the contradictory consequences of a certain kind of introspective contemplation—namely, the vanishing of the I-sense into its objects. As is his frequent practice, Wittgenstein also mentions a second line of argument that is more logical and linguistic (an argument that may be of broader relevance, since it would also apply to forms of solipsism that may be more dependent on logical or transcendental forms of argument and less bound up with a particular attitude or lived context). He points out that a statement such as "this experience is *my* experience" is, from a logical point of view, essentially empty or meaningless (tautologous), since its negation is not false but inconceivable. Such a sentence could have meaning only if it were at least conceivable that my experience could belong to some other consciousness. For, "if as a matter of logic you exclude other people's having something, it loses its sense to say that you have it" (PI, §398).

One paradoxical implication can be drawn from both the phenomenological and the linguistic arguments. It seems that the solipsist must, in the very act of declaring his own unique, constituting centrality, necessarily presuppose and invoke (at an implicit level, often not realized even by himself) a contradictory insight, the existence of one or more other minds or conscious centers. According to the linguistic argument, when the solipsist utters sentences such as "this experience is my experience," he must, on pain of mouthing a blatant tautology, be sneaking in the assumption that things could have been different, that other consciousnesses might have possessed *his* experiences. But all this assumes that other consciousnesses do exist. And, as we have seen, the phenomenological argument shows that, from within, the solipsist's consciousness dissolves into its world since it has no existence apart from its objects. If the solipsist nevertheless *has* an experience of the existence of *his* own consciousness, this must be because he is implicitly adopting a perspective from *without*—the standpoint of some other consciousness who can take the solipsist's consciousness as its object. Wittgenstein thus shows that, if the solipsist is to hold onto his basic insight of the centrality of his own consciousness, then he cannot just *have* experiences; he must in some way *experience* his experiences, and this implies projecting himself into an external position—a vantage point he imaginatively occupies while still experiencing it as other and alien.

It seems that, to remain a solipsist, the solipsist must inevitably waver between two unstable positions. When he concentrates on observing his own experiences, the solipsistic revelation of centrality disappears as the I-sense dissolves (thus denying the existence of the solipsistic self). But if he persists in holding to the solipsistic revelation, insisting on its meaningfulness and importance, he necessarily invokes a contradictory presupposition, a world in which at least one other consciousness exists to serve as an alternative to his own consciousness, or to take his own consciousness as an object. The implication is certainly paradoxical: solipsism, strangely enough, seems to demand an other mind.[27]

In Wittgenstein's view, then, solipsism as a philosophical position is either empty or self-contradictory. Its central intuition, the seemingly bold and shocking claim of the absolute epistemological centrality of the self, either dissolves, by reducing to the truism that what is experienced is what is experienced, or else self-destructs, by assuming its own contradiction. But if solipsism leads to a "no-ownership doctrine" or the postulation of an other mind, then the aggrandizement and diminishment of the self are not polar opposites after all: the one transforms naturally enough into the other. Further, both are embedded in the same experiential stance—a passive hyperawareness that places the world at a distance and subjectivizes it, while stripping experience of all sense of active engagement. Let us now return to the lived-world of Schreber, with its classic examples of core schizophrenic-type symptoms. In his experiences of losing a sense of selfhood, or of being watched or controlled, one finds the existential counterparts of the logical self-contradictions of the metaphysical doctrine of solipsism.

As we have seen, Schreber's feeling of being the conscious center of the world was continually transforming into its opposite. As he sat or stood without moving, he was as likely to experience a loss of self (a feeling that his thoughts were being thought by some other subjectivity or by no one at all) as to sense his own ontological centrality. "Seeing" only happens here, he felt—but he also felt that there was no "I": experience belonged to an other who was always elsewhere, or it floated free of all selfhood altogether. Schreber before the mirror, experiencing himself as "represented-as" female, thus exemplifies the condition and the paradox of solipsism. Here we have a man standing still, staring rigidly at a world that is, quite literally, a reflection of himself and a projection of his own mind (the feminized seeing-as), yet who, at this very instant, fails to recognize that the world before his eyes, a world he feels *as* subjectivized, is the product of his own consciousness. "I am represented as a woman," says Schreber—as if all vestiges of his I-sense had disappeared into the objects of his awareness, and the source of consciousness now resided in some other place or else nowhere at all.

In those other moments when Schreber *did* feel himself to be a knowing center who owned the experiential world looming before him, we see solipsism contradicting itself by postulating a second consciousness. In line with Wittgenstein's argument, these experiences seem to have occurred only when Schreber felt the presence of an alien awareness who could take Schreber's experience as *its* object—that is, when he was experiencing some of the classic first-rank symptoms of schizophrenia. For, as we saw in several examples above, Schreber's very experience of owning his experiences, or of recognizing his experiences as experiences (both aspects of his being-as-constituting-consciousness), existed from the perspective of an other—the "one" who thought that the ideas in a book or newspaper were Schreber's own, or the "one" who saw that Schreber had seen a butterfly. Oddly enough (but also, as Wittgenstein shows, predictably enough), Schreber's sense of being a solipsistic center occurred at those very moments when he was also experiencing the contradictory presence of an other mind.

THE PHILOSOPHER'S SIN

In Wittgenstein's view, to insist on the truism of solipsism is to engage in a form of life that is self-deceptive, futile, and ultimately absurd. He calls the "private experience," at least as this is conceived within the tradition of Cartesian philosophy, a "degenerate construction of our grammar (comparable in a sense to tautology and contradiction)," and he compares the solipsist to a man who thinks he can make an automobile move faster by pushing against its dashboard from within (NFL, 314; BBB, 71). Caught up in the intensity and seriousness of his own scrutinizing effort, the solipsist forgets that he has enclosed himself in a separate world, thus cutting himself off from any possibility of effective action, of real discovery, or of meaningful communication with his fellow human beings.

Wittgenstein's phenomenological and linguistic analyses are meant to provide insight into the curious nature of solipsistic assertions so that those who intend to be solipsists can be brought to see that there is nothing coherent they intend to say. As a young man he had been powerfully attracted to the philosophy of Schopenhauer, a form of epistemological idealism which, for him at least, contained a strong hint of solipsism.[28] "As regards Solipsism and Idealism," reports G. E. Moore, Wittgenstein "said that he himself had been often tempted to say 'All that is real is the experience of the present moment' or 'All that is certain is the experience of the present moment' . . . [or] 'The only reality is *my* present experience'" (L,15); and in the notebooks Wittgenstein kept in his mid-twenties are lines such as this: "As my idea is the world, in the same way my will is the world-will" (NB, 85). Wittgenstein's later philosophical thought involves a reaction against this temptation he knew very well, a temptation toward mental solitude and withdrawal that lasted throughout his life and whose affinities with the delusions of insanity he mentioned more than once.[29] It is always significant, Iris Murdoch has written, to ask of a philosopher: What is he afraid of?[30] I would argue that what Wittgenstein most feared was something akin to the madness that afflicted Schreber, and that his philosophy is motivated, at least in part, by a strenuous attempt to ward off such a mode of existence.

In making this point, I am, of course, not attempting to gainsay the philosophical value and validity of the work of Ludwig Wittgenstein. As philosophical contributions, his arguments and analyses stand on their own and must ultimately be assessed independently of the issue of personal motivations. Still, it is interesting to note that Wittgenstein did have a persistent fear of madness, a madness that was hardly unrelated to his own temptations toward the lonely rigors of philosophical thought. Bertrand Russell, who knew the younger Wittgenstein very well, describes him as a person so preoccupied with thinking as to have been on the verge of actual madness, a person who often complained that logic was driving him into insanity.[31] Wittgenstein writes of this fear in his more personal, nonphilosophical notes, which contain the line used as an epigraph for this work, "in the health of our intellect we are surrounded by madness," as well as this frank admission: "I am often afraid of madness"—a condition he associates with loneliness or isolation, with becoming "inaccessible," "withdrawn," and "devoid of love" (CV, 44, 53, 54).

So it is particularly interesting to realize that Wittgenstein often spoke of his own philosophical thought—a kind of antiphilosophy—as an attempt to restore sanity and health to the mind caught up with certain abstract dilemmas and disengaged attitudes typical of philosophy of a more metaphysical sort. "What has to be explained is this," he once wrote, "Why do we talk to our impression?" (BBB, 177). He wanted to call philosophers back from the conversations they were having with their private impressions and abstract concepts, and from all the delusions and doubts such conversations engender, thereby to place them squarely back in the practical and communal discourse of life. Though solipsism was the major instance of an alienating philosophical illusion, it was not the only one. Other famous examples, which Wittgenstein also associated with the attitude of passive staring, include the problem of skepticism, of a "private language," and the "essentialistic" illusion (the latter to be discussed in Chapter 3).

Wittgenstein's image of pushing the dashboard from within a car is but one of many striking metaphors by which he expressed a certain notion of futility. His writings are in fact filled with such images: engines idling in neutral, a person talking to himself, words looked up in the imagination, business transactions conducted between the right and left hands of a single person, a cogwheel that turns without connecting with any other part of a machine, clocks whose faces are attached to their hands, someone who goes through the motions of weaving while sitting at an empty loom (PI, §§132, 260–71, 414; BBB, 71). The common theme is the absurdity and emptiness that result when self-reference precludes engagement with a world outside the self. For Wittgenstein, it is this failure to connect with a practical and social world that is a sort of original sin of the intellect—the philosopher's sin par excellence, of which solipsism is but the most blatant example.

Still, as Wittgenstein knew very well, demonstrating the logical impossibility and incoherence of solipsism as a philosophical doctrine can hardly preclude its existence in the actual world, both as an explicitly held belief (philosophical solipsism proper) and as an implicitly felt mood (what I am calling quasi-solipsism). Wittgenstein himself insisted that, despite their absurdity and logical incoherence, sentences like "the only reality is the present experience" and "the only reality is *my* present experience" do correspond to something of enormous importance in human life, a profound metaphysical intuition about the experiencing self's centrality in relation to its world (L, 15). And, he seemed to think, although this intuition could not really be *said* (because it was nonsensical, tautologous), it could in some sense be *shown*—by pointing to the mood, attitude, or form of life in which the doctrine is rooted.[32] Virtually the whole of the present book has been an attempt to do this kind of showing, by tracing the existential origins and implications of Schreber's quasi-solipsism and demonstrating parallels with Wittgenstein's phenomenology of philosophical error. We have found, throughout, that even the contradictions that undermine or invalidate solipsism as a coherent philosophical position are central features of quasi-solipsism as a mode of experience.

ON CONTRADICTION

A careful reading of the *Memoirs* reveals that Schreber does more than merely manifest the contradictions of self-consciousness, the paradoxes of the reflexive, as they might be called. He is also at least dimly aware of these contradictions that show up in his relationship to God and the world. Thus he realizes that certain inconsistencies imbue what might be called his metaphysical account of God's nature and role; and he even seems to recognize that these inconsistencies (rather like those of Wittgenstein's solipsist) stem from his having, at different times, experiences that are equally compelling though mutually contradictory. In one footnote from the *Memoirs*, for example, after referring to the issue of whether God is fundamentally ignorant and mistaken in his understanding of human nature, Schreber writes, "Earlier . . . I stated the contrary opinion. This is because these matters, by their very nature, make any absolutely final opinion impossible; hence I vacillate even now as new impressions seem to favour first one conception and then the other" (M, 198n).[33]

In another passage Schreber muses on the strange, almost incomprehensible fact that God—who by definition is the supreme being, defined by his omnipotence and omniscience—"should here [in the *Memoirs*] be depicted as so lowly a Being that He can be surpassed both morally and mentally by one single human being [namely, by Schreber himself]." Even stranger is Schreber's way of qualifying this self-aggrandizing claim: "my superiority [to God]," he writes, "is to be understood in *the most relative sense*" [in *ganz relativem Sinne*]—that is to say, only insofar "as it concerns the condition contrary to the Order of the World originating from permanent and indissoluble nerve contact with one single human being" (M, 155). This reference to the aberrant condition of exclusive "nerve contact" is an allusion to the essential solipsism of Schreber's universe, a universe where he is the only "seer" (and God's only conduit). Schreber himself seems to feel somewhat uncertain and confused about what he is getting at here (in a footnote to this passage he speaks of encountering questions that are "among the thorniest problems since thinking human beings have existed"; M, 155n). Yet it seems clear enough that he is also, in some sense, relativizing his solipsism, and the grandiosity it implies (his superiority to God)—as if he had somehow managed to stand *outside* his solipsism and recognize its truths as being relevant only from within.

Awareness of contradiction also shows up in Schreber's speculations about the origins of the cosmos and of human beings. He is aware, on the one hand, of what he calls "spontaneous generation" or "divine miracles," the solipsistic process (Schreber carefully distinguishes it from generation "in the materialistic sense") in which beings are willed to come into existence for him alone and before his privileged gaze (M, 183–86). But, Schreber wonders, if creation depends in some sense on his gaze (as is suggested by this spontaneous creation), how then could he himself, *with* his gaze, have been created? Perplexed by the riddle, Schreber states that the creation of "a complete human being" (Schreber himself, the only real conscious center) must have been something "exceptional," requiring "an extraordinary exertion of power." Indeed, "as a permanent state of affairs, this [creation of a complete human being, i.e., a constituting center] was probably incompatible with the needs of the rest of the universe, perhaps even incompatible with the very existence of God himself" (M, 184). For, as he puts it elsewhere in the *Memoirs*, "one" was apparently not inclined "to put up with the idea of being dependent on a single human being whom one would otherwise have looked down upon in the proud awareness of distant power" (M, 140).[34]

In such passages Schreber seems to be writhing in the coils of an epistemic/ontological paradox—endlessly shifting between two interdependent yet incompatible visions, the experience of his own consciousness as both a constituted object and the ultimate, constituting subject. The enigmatic, vexed nature of the *Memoirs* testifies to Schreber's inability either to solve these dilemmas or to ignore them.

In one passage from the *Memoirs*, in which Schreber describes hearing a series of phrases and sentences that are "spoken through my head as it were" (M, 152), his awareness of the essential paradoxicality of his lived-world reaches a kind of crescendo. Some of the phrases he hears appear to express his feeling of being a constituting center, as when one god chides another: "well, since you have made the weather dependent on one human being's thoughts." But other phrases "spoken through his head" express the other side of his quasi-solipsistic world, the sense of being a mere figment, created by and at the mercy of an all-powerful other mind. Thus, he tells of how these speaking gods address him: "On a very few occasions one even went so far as to make a kind of confession of one's own guilt; for instance: 'If only *I* had not put you among the fleeting-improvised men' . . . or 'What is to become of the whole cursed affair', or 'If only the cursed play-with-human-beings would cease'." Schreber also heard "talk of 'colossal powers' on the part of God's omnipotence and of 'hopeless resistance' on my part" (M, 151–52).

Still other phrases can be read as more direct and general declarations of the absurdity or impossibility of a solipsistic world: "All nonsense (that is, the nonsense of thought reading and falsifying thoughts) cancels itself out. . . . Don't forget that all representing is nonsense. . . . Don't forget that the end of the world is a contradiction in itself" (M, 151–52).[35]

Schreber refers to these phrases as containing "a tangle of contradictions which cannot be unravelled" because of the "insufficiency of the human apparatus for comprehension." For, he declares, "almost insuperable difficulties arise even for me at every attempt to solve these contradictions; a really satisfactory solution would only be possible if one had such complete insight into the nature of God which not even I have attained who have certainly gained deeper insight than all other human beings, because human capacity is limited" (M, 152–53).

Clearly, a quasi-solipsism like Schreber's is fraught with contradiction. To some readers, however, this very quality might seem to undermine my general line of argument. Tolerance of contradiction is, after all, a central feature of the most immature primary-process thought, with its lack of critical, self-reflective awareness and its domination by the irrationality of the id.[36] Have I ended up, then, by demonstrating the very characteristics of schizophrenia that traditional psychoanalytic interpretations have been emphasizing all along?

This objection is important, not least because of an unspoken presupposition embedded in it: the equation of contradiction with the irrational, the instinctual, and the primitive. Such an assumption may have made some readers dubious from the outset about the very idea of a comparison between philosophy and madness. But Wittgenstein's insights suggest another way of understanding certain contradictions, in philosophy as well as in life. Many strange and paradoxical characteristics of schizophrenia can arise from *within* aspects of experience traditionally equated with maturity and health: from disengagement, self-consciousness, and capacity for reflective distance—all of which are antithetical to any notion of primitivity or the "primary process."

We have seen that certain lived contradictions arise from Schreber's standing apart from the vital flow of life, from the distanced, observational stance he adopts toward his own experience-as-such. True, he appears to lack critical self-consciousness about the *effects* of this stance (even though, as we have seen, he does have some awareness of the contradictions involved); but this lack is clearly at a much higher developmental level than that of the infant or young child, with their relatively unreflective, instinct-dominated thought. For what Schreber fails to recognize are the effects of a hyper-self-consciousness that is already in place, constituting a lived-world that is far from Dionysian or primitive. It would be misleading to assume that Schreber could be cured if only he could manage another cognitive act of distancing, a further distancing from the distancing inherent in the hyper-self-consciousness of his quasi-solipsism. What Schreber lacks is not the observing ego emphasized by ego psychologists[37] but, instead, a fundamental rootedness in the lived-body and the consensual and practical world. Without such rootedness, even a Wittgensteinian awareness of the sources and contradictions of solipsism could have little real effect, one suspects; this too would exist as something merely ideational or hypothetical, as a mere thought experiment, so to speak.

There would, however, be some validity to saying that such a solipsist's overvaluation of a contemplative stance indicates a lack of a sense of proportion, a failure to put the cognitive in its place. But if one wished to compare this to a developmental stage, it would seem closest to the special kind of "egocentricity" that the developmental psychologist Jean Piaget sees as characteristic of the adolescent, who overemphasizes thought at the expense of the practical world. And this, in turn, might help to explain why schizophrenia does not have its onset before adolescence—the stage of cognitive development when so-called formal operations, the capacity to think about thought, first develop, and one comes to be aware of one's own consciousness and its role in constituting the world. Could we, perhaps, think of a lived-world like Schreber's as the dark side of Piagetian formal operations?

But richer and, I think, more revealing comparisons can be drawn with a stage or period in cultural history, one in which the role of contradiction or paradox emerges with particular force. There are, in fact, remarkable affinities between schizophrenic forms of experience and expression and the art, literature, and thought of the modernist and so-called postmodernist age.[38] These issues are complex, and to explore them in real detail would take us far afield. Still, some brief consideration of this epoch and its attendant contradictions is worthwhile: it offers a larger context in which to understand the paradoxes that preoccupied both Wittgenstein and Schreber and, perhaps, can help to account for the striking convergence of their concerns.

DUALITIES OF MODERN THOUGHT

The relevant paradoxes of modern thought and consciousness receive their most intriguing exposition at the end of the philosopher-historian Michel Foucault's remarkable book, *The Order of Things*, where Foucault identifies the advent of the modern mode of thought and self-knowledge, what he calls the modern *episteme*, with the innovations of Kantian philosophy. It was Kant who decisively introduced a new kind of self-consciousness, a dual self-consciousness in which human subjectivity came to be understood—and potentially, experienced—as, at the same time, both a knowing subject and a primary object of knowing. With his notion of the "categories of understanding," the fundamental forms of organization—temporal, spatial, and causal—to which all human experience must necessarily conform, Kant emphasized the transcendental role of the mind in constituting the world we experience. At the same time his self-reflexive focus on the categories also had the effect of turning subjectivity into a prime object of study, an empirical entity that would itself be investigated by newly developing human sciences that aspired to specify the nature or explain the sources of these very categories or cultural forms. This new duality of human self-awareness had some peculiar implications and consequences.

For one thing, it led to certain contradictions that threatened to undermine the entire project of reflective self-understanding that Kant had initiated. After all, if subjectivity is conceived in transcendental terms, as the medium by which everything is known or in which it has its being, how then can subjectivity itself ever *be* known? Would this not require the impossible: that subjectivity should turn around on itself, becoming an object within its own field, within the medium that it itself is? Foucault describes the human sciences of the modern *episteme* as suffering from a "confusion of the empirical and the transcendental." Because they treat "as their object what is in fact their condition of possibility," these sciences are doomed to certain "warped and twisted forms of reflection"—to futile contortions of thought that will continually evoke, yet continually frustrate, the hope for some profound insight into subjectivity and its relationship to the world.[39]

A second consequence of the Kantian duality, of what Foucault calls the doublet of modern thought, is a certain polarization or duality in the status of human consciousness and, potentially, in the individual person's sense of self. If human consciousness is in some way the source or foundation of all reality (or, at least, of all reality that can possibly be of relevance to beings such as ourselves), then consciousness, or the human self, might seem to hold a position of ultimate sovereignty and omniscience. Yet, if consciousness has also come to be the object of new disciplines that seek to understand its causes and processes of functioning, it is also being assimilated to the natural order of determined entities. Far from being sovereign, mind is discovered to be constrained by all the rules of material causality, biological law, and historical process. Schopenhauer described what he termed this "two-fold nature of . . . consciousness"—the antinomy whereby consciousness, the "supporter of the world, the universal condition of all that appears," also recognizes itself to be merely a "modification of matter," thus to be "just as necessarily wholly dependent upon a long chain of causes and effects which have preceded it, and in which it itself appears as a small link." He describes a curious coexistence of, or oscillation between, feelings of nothing and of ultimate centrality: "Every individual, completely vanishing and reduced to nothing in a boundless world, nevertheless makes himself the center of the world."[40] Further, the very idea of forms of knowing or categories of understanding tends to deflate any pretensions to omniscience, for this idea suggests that consciousness has certain limits: though its domain may feel immense, without visible boundary, it must also seem narrow, for now one is likely to recognize at least the abstract possibility of inconceivable realities whose very nature excludes them from comprehension by the human mind.

Here, then, are the dual results of Kantian reflection, an introverted process whose effect, in Hegel's words, is "to withdraw cognition from an interest in its objects and absorption in the study of them, and to direct it back upon itself."[41] To the extent that one focuses on the world, the world feels subjectivized, even subordinate to one's will; but to the extent that one focuses on one's own mind or thinking, consciousness itself begins to seem at a remove, alien and constrained. So consciousness in the post-Kantian age becomes something profoundly ambiguous: all-powerful and all-knowing (a kind of deity that thinks the world) but also objectlike and finite—determined, knowable, as well as limited in its capacity *to* know.

Ludwig Wittgenstein can be viewed as a major critic but also, in some respects, an important exemplar of these paradoxical trends of the modern *episteme*. It is not that he was exclusively concerned with forms of illusion and contradiction peculiar to this age: some of his points certainly involve more general criticisms of the abstract and isolated intellect, of consciousness removed from practical reality and the conventions of social intercourse (and these points also apply to such major premodern figures as Plato or Saint Augustine). But he did have a special intimacy with and concern for the paradoxes of self-reflection, for the condition of the modern, introverted mind, with its propensity for grandiosity as well as paranoia and self-undermining doubt.

Wittgenstein's interest in philosophy began, in fact, with a fascination with certain paradoxes of the reflexive, logical paradoxes generated by the prospect of self-reference (of sentences) or self-inclusion (of sets). This interest culminated in his early, enigmatic masterpiece, the *Tractatus Logico-Philosophicus*—a work on logic and language that simultaneously criticizes and continues the Kantian project, while flaunting the self-contradictions this entails. The *Tractatus* articulates the logical impossibility, the utter nonsensicality, of any attempt to carry out the modernist project of describing the all-encompassing limits or structures of thought or the general relationship between language and the world. To do this, however, Wittgenstein's book lays out a general theory of what *can* be said (namely, only statements that describe concatenations of facts within the world); and this means—as Wittgenstein well knew—that his book was participating in the very project (clearly a post-Kantian project) of attempting to articulate the limits of human knowledge even as it presented a philosophical semantics that would preclude any such articulation as impossible.

Wittgenstein's concern with the central illusions and paradoxes of modern reflexivity remained equally central in his later work. Then, however, he attempted to disown the more extreme (in a sense, Kantian) ambitions of reflective self-awareness that had animated the *Tractatus*, replacing these with what seems a more humble, antimetaphysical enterprise of philosophical critique and dissolution. He, at least, considered this therapeutic antiphilosophizing to be profoundly at odds with the modern world, a civilization whose spirit he described as "alien and uncongenial" and which he compared to "the unimpressive spectacle of a crowd whose best members work for purely private ends" (CV, 6). Though Wittgenstein's most explicit criticisms of the modern era focused on its scientism and worship of technology, he also had a deep concern with modern conceptions of consciousness and of knowledge—and implicitly, I would argue, with the forms of experience that mimic these conceptions, forms with which he appears to have had considerable personal familiarity. Wittgenstein seems, for example, to have had a special animus against the two sides of the modern conception of the mind, for he set himself equally against all tendencies either to reduce everything to subjectivity or the self or, alternatively, to treat consciousness or the self as any kind of thing.[42] The two paradoxes discussed in this chapter suggest a related set of concerns. In criticizing the dual understanding of indexicals or shifter words such as "here," and in showing that the solipsist's sense of centrality depends on simultaneously adopting an imaginary or external viewpoint, Wittgenstein is bringing out the kind of contradiction that is implicit in what Foucault calls the empirico-transcendental doublet of modern thought: he shows that the sense of the absolutely transcendental role played by one's own consciousness is, in fact, inseparable from and dependent on one's also focusing on consciousness as an empirical or objectifiable entity.

Wittgenstein always struggled with the self-contradictory modern urge to give an explicit statement of the transcendental limits of meaningfulness or of experience, an attempt that leads to a characteristic shifting between omniscience and ignorance, to a paradoxical sense of one's knowing as simultaneously all-encompassing yet exclusionary. He knew that to give such a statement required a self-contradictory and impossible act, that of standing outside, and objectifying, the very structures of one's own knowing or speaking. Though it is unlikely Wittgenstein ever managed to evade this (perhaps ineluctable) contradiction of modern thought, it is clear enough that it is an issue of which he was acutely aware.

The dualities and contradictions endemic to modern thought are strikingly akin to those we have identified in schizophrenia—another condition in which the mind turns away from others and the world to become preoccupied with itself. Schizophrenic patients, too, tend to oscillate between, or even to combine, a sense of tremendous, somehow cosmic grandiosity and feelings of abject powerlessness and ignorance. They too are as likely to feel they have limitless power over events as to feel the opposite, that even their actions and, especially, their very thoughts are under the surveillance or control of outside forces; indeed, they can have these seemingly contradictory feelings in rapid oscillation or at the very same moment.

Thus, Schreber sometimes experienced either his delusional objects or both his real and his delusional objects as being unreal, existing only for him, the source of all "seeing"; but he could also experience his mind as an object contemplated or even manipulated by some encompassing other mind. Schreber's paradoxical condition is also manifest in his key notion of "divine miracles" or "spontaneous generation," the process whereby beings appear in his immediate vicinity. Although he treats this process as an event that happens *in* the world (a rather mysterious, nonmaterialistic event, but an event nonetheless; e.g., M, 185–86), there is, at the same time, the strong implication that this appearing-event is not just an event among others but, in some sense, the transcendental source of everything. As Schreber himself tells us, "seeing . . . is confined to my person and immediate surroundings," and "everything that happens is in reference to me"; "I became

. . . the only human being, or simply the human being around whom everything turns" (M, 232, 197). And so, what Foucault says of the modern mind applies equally to Schreber: he too treats as an object what is in fact the very condition of all being or appearing; in both cases, "what is given in experience and what renders experience possible correspond to one another in an endless oscillation."[43]

Schreber also displays a characteristic veering between omniscience and ignorance that is reminiscent of Foucault's remarks on the "vast but narrow space" opened up by modern consciousness, that "difficult object and sovereign subject of all possible knowledge."[44] Schreber claims, on the one hand, that "insight into the true state of divine matters"—including the matter of "spontaneous generation," mind making the world—was granted him "in an incomparably higher degree than any other human being before"; he even goes so far as to place his own knowledge and mental capacity above that of God (M, 289, 155). On the other hand, he also conceives his mind as blinkered and constrained. Remember that Schreber's "superiority," as he himself tells us, applies only "in the most relative sense." Further, he says, "my personal experiences enable me to lift the veil only partially"; "After all I too am only a human being and therefore limited by the confines of human understanding" (M, 155, 54, 41).

As we know, Schreber was hardly insensitive to these profound contradictions of his experience. Indeed, his awareness of them recalls Wittgenstein's critical analyses of solipsism and other philosophical illusions as well as Foucault's remarks about the "warped and twisted forms of reflection" characteristic of the modern, self-regarding mind. As Schreber's hallucinatory voices suggest, central features of his solipsistic, involuted universe—"representing," "thought reading," "the end of the world"—seem at times to be nonsensical, self-cancelling; each, say the voices, is a "contradiction in itself." There is no doubt that Schreber himself recognized the oddity as well as the immense complexity and almost impenetrable obscurity of his world, for he describes it as "out-of-joint," as a "miraculous structure" or "miraculous organization" that has "suffered a rent, intimately connected with my personal fate," and he characterizes it as "the most difficult subject ever to exercise the human mind" (M, 54, 184).

Here, then, are the central paradoxes of schizophrenic existence; they suggest a profound kinship with the core dilemmas of the reflexive—and the modern—soul.[45]

3

A VAST MUSEUM OF STRANGENESS

To live in the world as if in a vast museum of strangeness . . .

—Giorgio de Chirico

In the Introduction and beginning of Chapter 1, I mentioned several characteristics of schizophrenic-type delusion that seemed inconsistent with the standard poor reality-testing and primitivity interpretations. In the course of the subsequent analysis, I considered most of these features, suggesting in each case that the characteristic in question is more consistent with the solipsistic interpretation of the schizophrenic world. Contrary to what Karl Jaspers's views may suggest, these aspects of the schizophrenic world do not exist beyond the pale of any possible comprehension.

Without reiterating the arguments already offered, let me simply list the features that have been described and interpreted in this light:

1. A certain irony on the patient's part about his or her own delusional world.

2. An attitude toward the delusional that is peculiarly inconsequent at times, often involving a "double bookkeeping" that separates the delusional from the real world.

3. A specific schizophrenic incorrigibility, that is, a sense of absolute certainty about the delusions. Added to features (2) and (3) is the

strange, seemingly paradoxical fact of their coexistence: the combination of incorrigibility with inconsequentiality for the realm of action.

4. Bizarre content that is not readily explicable as wish-fulfillment fantasy, since the delusions involve not mere exaggerations but radical transformations of the normal human form of life—in particular, profound distortions of the feeling of ownership of or control over the self (e.g., certain of Schneider's first-rank symptoms); of the separateness, reality, or solidity of the external world; and of the sense that other human beings possess consciousness.

5. Illusions of inauthenticity and delusions of disbelief (about the real or consensual world).

Also, in Chapter 2 I focused on two aspects of schizophrenic delusion that seemed, at least at first, to contradict the purported solipsism: first, a tendency for what would seem to be solipsistic or quasi-solipsistic claims to pertain nevertheless to the objective or consensual world; second, a tendency for schizophrenics to experience themselves as being in the presence, or at the mercy, of some all-powerful or all-knowing other mind.

I turn now to certain "atmospheric" qualities that are, perhaps, the most subtle and difficult to grasp of all aspects of schizophrenia. I have already considered, at the end of Chapter 1, the strange combination of an absence of emotional resonance with a profound, omnipresent, somehow abstract anxiety—an anxiety born of feeling that, as one schizophrenic put it, "the world must be represented or the world will disappear."[1] Two other atmospheric qualities have not yet been examined, however. The first of these is a nearly inexpressible quality that R. D. Laing once termed "phantom concreteness," a feeling of almost material actuality characterizing what might be expected to have a more ephemeral and inner mode of being. The second quality is even more difficult to describe, for patient as well as psychologist. In this experience, which I call "mute particularity" or "uncanny particularity," the perceptual world takes on a certain overwhelming but ineffable feeling of specificity, particularity, or exactness—so that objects and events come to seem fraught with uncanny meaning and, in some instances, to feel like copies, exemplifications, or repetitions of themselves. The latter accounts, in large part, for the "subtle, pervasive and strangely uncertain light" and the sense of uncanny tension of what Jaspers calls the true "delusional atmosphere."[2]

PHANTOM CONCRETENESS

Phantom concreteness is the rather contradictory tendency for consciousness to be experienced as something inner that nevertheless has a certain feeling of concrete, almost material actuality.[3] This mode of experience involves an at least quasi-solipsistic tendency to concentrate attention on one's own inner experiences, yet it undermines the original solipsistic impulse in a couple of ways: it deprives the content of experience of certain qualities of the mental or the subjective while at the same time undermining the self's sense of epistemological centrality. Once again it is useful to consider Wittgenstein's critique of related developments in philosophical thought; this time, however, I alter the strategy of presentation, beginning with his critique of philosophy and only then proceeding to analyze the experience of patients.

Wittgenstein criticizes the tendency of philosophers to reify experiences in the course of their analyses. An especially common and influential example is the philosophical doctrine of sense data, a doctrine that asserts the existence of a special middle world of experiences that are, at the same time, private or inner yet also object-like, somehow substantial. This model of mind is well illustrated in Hume, who wrote, "We have no perfect idea of substance; but taking it for *something that can exist by itself*, 'tis evident every perception is a substance."[4] In Wittgenstein's view, taking such a position is analogous to treating the experience of pain in the statement "I have toothache" as if it were equivalent in ontological status to the objects referred to in a statement like "I have five shillings"—as if the pain were really like a material object except for being somehow inner or private (NFL, 302). Wittgenstein's argument against such a way of thinking is complex, and it does not amount to a behavioristic denial of the reality or importance of the experiential dimension of life. His point is not to question the lived reality of such experiences as those of pain but to criticize the philosopher's tendency to reify these experiences by conceiving of them as sharply defined, distinct, and substantialized entities which, though inner, somehow seem to exist independently of the experiencing subject. "You have a new conception and interpret it as seeing a new object," writes Wittgenstein of this self-deluding philosophical move. "You interpret a grammatical movement made by yourself as a quasi-physical phenomenon which you are observing. (Think for example of the question: 'Are sense-data the material of which the universe is made?')" (PI, §401). In this way experience can come to be imagined as something objectlike and at a distance, "almost like something painted on a screen which surrounds me" (NFL, 311).

In the sway of this picture of human consciousness, says Wittgenstein, philosophers often begin to ask unnecessary and unanswerable questions: for example, Is it possible for me to experience *your* pain?—a question which presupposes that your pain is an entity that might be passed to me, like a marble or a photograph. Wittgenstein argues that such thinglike mental states do not exist, except as artifacts of reflection, conceptual postulates for philosophers or psychologists who reflect on experience (or concentrate their attention on experience) but who have lost touch with the lived reality of prereflective existence. Because they yearn to understand this inner dimension on the analogy of the (presumably better understood) things of the external world (e.g., by thinking of sense data as something like electrons; BBB, 70), such thinkers get themselves into all sorts of unnecessary philosophical quandaries; and they foster a seductive but misleading picture of the nature of human experience, a picture that has been quite dominant in Western thought since the time of Descartes.

Part of the blame for this misleading reification can be placed on language, with its tendency to label processes by means of substantive terms. But Wittgenstein also suggests that, like solipsism itself (with which he considers it closely allied), this kind of reification is bound up with the phenomenon of staring (NFL, 309, 311, 315; PI, §398). Thus, the passive and detached concentration involved in scrutinizing experience-as-such involves a certain distancing from, and it brings on a substantializing of, whatever is taken as the object of awareness. The ensuing transformation or distortion is clearest in cases in which the original object of awareness is an abstraction, or where it is subjectivity itself.

Particularly clear examples of such reification or substantialization can be found in the purported findings of classical introspectionist psychologists such as E. B. Titchener, whose method of observation involved the bracketing out of the real world (thus avoiding what he called the "stimulus-error") in favor of a scrutinizing description of experience or sensation as such. What Wittgenstein would dismiss as artifacts of an artificial and distorting method Titchener thought of as discoveries. Thus, by means of his introspectionist method, he claimed to have refuted the claim, made by psychologists of the Würzburg school, that thought could occur in the absence of sensory imagery. Titchener argued that even the meanings of the most abstract notions were always mediated by concrete, substancelike images. He claimed, for example, to have discovered, by careful introspection, that his own understanding of the meaning of "meaning"—that most ephemeral and abstract of concepts—was actually carried by the image of "the blue-grey tip of a kind of scoop, which has a bit of yellow above it (presumably a part of the handle), and which is just digging into a dark mass of what appears to be plastic material." Even the meaning of "this is abstract" was mediated by some image, such as "a closed visual pattern" or "an overarching dome." Titchener was convinced that other people would find imagery of similar sensory specificity, if only they too properly carried out the task of what he called "hard introspective labor."[5]

Titchener also "discovered" that the act of will, the inner feeling of exercising volition, was nothing more than an epiphenomenon of kinesthetic sensations and other sensory images that have a quasi-external, quasi-substantialized quality. What other schools of psychology would consider to be powers, faculties, acts, or functions of the mind were reduced by Titchener to certain elements found (by introspection) within the contents of the mind; even the sense of self was essentially constituted by kinesthetic and visceral sensations.[6] Using a similar type of introspection, William James concluded that the senses of volition and of selfhood were in fact reducible to a "collection of . . . peculiar motions in the head or between the head and throat" and that "all that is experienced is, strictly considered, *objective,*" even that "imaginary being denoted by the pronoun 'I'." In the *Philosophical Investigations,* Wittgenstein criticizes such instances of introspection, in one passage addressing himself specifically to James. In Wittgenstein's view, James's introspection fails to show or analyze what is normally meant by the word "self"; rather, it reveals something highly artificial: "the state of a philosopher's attention when he says the word 'self' to himself and tries to analyse its meaning" (PI, §413).[7]

In criticizing such philosophical concepts, Wittgenstein is concerned with their aptness as descriptions of the modes of experience characteristic of normal, engaged life, where mental processes are lived as but the transparent medium through which external objects are experienced. Here the reifying philosophical language of sense data and mental objects does seem to distort the true nature of such experience. Wittgenstein does not mention, however, that there are also lived-worlds which seem to be the existential counterparts to those philosophical worlds that reify the inner and the mental. This, in my opinion, is the case with hyperreflexive schizoid and schizophrenic patients who attend so intently to their mental processes and other experiences that they transform them, with the result that these processes actually come to *be* more like states or things. In such a lived-world, consciousness phenomena, through the very act of being seen, are substantialized into objectlike entities. (It is also possible for alterations in the quality of perceptions to incite a scrutinizing mode of attention, a mode that then proceeds to heighten these alterations further.)[8] Although these pseudo-entities are still, in one sense, mental and inner, they also come to have a certain felt externality, with the experiencing subject no longer dwelling in them but instead encountering them almost like independent objects. Further, these pseudo-entities take on that strange phenomenal presence, the bizarre combination of unreality and specificity, of the mental and the seemingly physical, called phantom concreteness.[9]

The schizophrenic patient Renée experienced her bodily sensations in an at least quasi-reified fashion. Her mouth, for example, sometimes felt as if it was "full of birds which I crunched between my teeth, and their feathers, their blood and broken bones were choking me." The images were, she wrote "so vivid that I experienced actual physical sensation." Other people often assumed that these vivid and seemingly literal descriptions indicated failures of reality-testing, as if Renée believed there actually were birds between her jaws. But, as Renée explained, she "readily distinguished" these quasi-external sensations from reality: "I can not say that I really saw images; they did not represent anything. Rather, I felt them."[10] Another schizophrenic person described his voices as seeming "about the size of a walnut"; others experienced their thoughts becoming visible, as if written in various letters or signs.[11] Schreber's *Memoirs* provide many similar examples of reified sensations. When he felt sensations in his body, for example, they were often substantialized and objectified. Pains in his head seemed to involve a "temporary thinning and furrowing of the bony substance of my skull" or the presence of "scorpions," "tiny crab- or spider-like structures"; in his arm he felt "a so-called 'large nerve' (a jelly-like mass about the size of a cherry)"; sensations in his eyelids were anthropomorphized as well as substantialized, becoming "little men" who occupied themselves with pulling his eyelids up and down with filaments as fine as cobwebs (M, 247, 99, 115, 136–38). Yet, all the while, he experienced these quasi-objects as existing only in the mind's eye—thus as a form of *phantom* concreteness.

Paradoxically enough, this very substantialization or concretization of images or sensations may encourage the person to feel that the experiences in question cannot possibly be mere products of his or her own consciousness. Thus, Schreber wrote of certain "visions [that] surpassed in their plasticity and photographic accuracy everything I had ever experienced when I was well" and concludes that "this cannot have been caused spontaneously by my own nerves, but must have been thrown into them by rays" (M, 81; for an example of such photographic specificity, see M, 193). Here we see how the attitude of staring, with its reifying concentration on inner experience-as-such, can obscure its own role in the constitution of experience, even encouraging belief in an other mind (since Schreber concluded that there must be rays who threw the visions into his nerves).[12] This combination of reification with alienation, of substantialization of inner sensory experiences with the feeling that one's own experiences are not really one's own, is particularly evident when it is the very act of perception that is objectified. Schreber writes of having felt a "soul" that "almost completely without thoughts and limited only to visual impressions, . . . started to join in searching when I was looking for some object in my environment, that is to say it joined in looking out of my eyes."[13] The presence of this soul "was felt as a sort of watery mass which covered my eyeballs" (M, 157). What seems to get reified here is not an object of experience, an inner sensation or image, but something closer to the act of seeing itself, which has come to feel both substantialized and alienated.

The phenomenon of phantom concreteness is perhaps even more bizarre when the reified experiences are not primarily sensory or perceptual but cerebral or intellectual, when what is seen in the mind's eye is the mind itself or even the mind in the very act of self-monitoring. This is the case with the nerves and rays that are so prominent in Schreber's delusional system. Careful reading of the *Memoirs* shows that these rays and nerves refer to two parts of Schreber's own, self-conscious mind: the part that watches, the rays; and the part that is watched, the nerves (at times Schreber also uses "nerves" in a generic sense, to refer to nerves *and* rays). Thus, the rays are constantly saying such things as "What are you thinking of now?" "Why don't you say it aloud?" or "Are you not ashamed, then?" as they hover over Schreber's more spontaneous inner thoughts, carried by the nerves and often expressed in what he calls a special "nerve language" (M, 69–70, 198–99). Within the solipsistic frame of his mind's eye world, Schreber seems to see a sort of second mind's eye, itself engaged in the act of contemplating his own consciousness or thoughts.

Here we are concerned with an aspect of experience that might be expected to be identified with the innermost self and to involve an abstract mode of experience far removed from anything sensory or physicalistic, namely, the act of self-consciousness itself. Yet Schreber is capable of describing the parts of his own mind and the relationship between these parts in the most concrete and externalized manner imaginable. The following passage, for example, must be read as a description of the psychological attraction exerted by his own thoughts on the self-monitoring part of his mind. (Elsewhere, in fact, Schreber tells us as much: the attraction exerted on the rays by the nerves should not be understood, he says, "in terms of natural forces acting purely mechanically [but as] something like a *psychological motive power*: the rays too find that 'attractive' which is of interest to them"; M, 48n.)[14] In the passage in question, Schreber describes what he refers to as "mechanical fastening" or "tying-to-rays"—a phenomenon of considerable sensory specificity whereby the rays, looking like a bundle of rods, hang together in a specific conelike formation in order to avoid being attracted through space toward the watched part of his own mind: "I can only describe the picture I saw with my mind's eye. According to this the souls [the rays] hung on a kind of bundle of rods (like the fasces of the Roman Lictors), but in such a manner that the rods spread out below like a cone, while the nerves of the souls were tied fast around the upper points" (M, 118).

Here, in the form of these rays and nerves, both aspects of Schreber's divided consciousness have come to be objects in his phenomenal field of awareness, with all the characteristics of perceptual objects that can be scrutinized and described. And this, I would argue, is closely analogous to what occurred when Titchener studied various attitudes of consciousness such as hesitation, vacillation, or dissent. Titchener claimed that, through his method of controlled scrutiny, one could discover that all these seemingly ephemeral and inner attitudes were always constituted by concrete, quasi-external phenomena. As Titchener put it, "All the [introspectionist] reports show the same features: visual images, pictorial or symbolic; internal speech; kinesthetic images; organic sensations. Nowhere a sign of the imageless component!"[15]

That consciousness seems to become perceptible does not, incidentally, contradict Wittgenstein's arguments, recounted in the previous chapter, about the necessary invisibility of the experiencing, transcendental, or solipsistic self. As we have seen, Schreber experiences consciousness as symbolized by the nerves and rays as a largely external being whom he watches from a remove, much as one might observe someone else speaking across a room; in Wittgenstein's metaphor quoted earlier, it is like seeing the farmer in the picture. Further, neither the rays nor the nerves function as *constituting* subjectivities in the moment they are seen: at times, Schreber even describes them as lacking thoughts, and the sentences they carry or convey sometimes lose all meaning and are experienced as meaningless, objectlike sound (M, 168–69, 234). The self-deceiving nature of this kind of reflexive vigilance is suggested by Schreber's failure to recognize these rays *as* manifestations of his own mind. The nerves and rays are seen from without, in the context of a more foundational mind's eye that encompasses them without itself being visible to the senses.[16] And so, the true nature of consciousness as constituting subjectivity is not represented, since the mind's eye, the currently constituting self or consciousness, remains invisible all the while. (Actually, the becoming visible of subjectivity itself is not quite so impossible as Wittgenstein's argument suggests; but, as we see in a few pages, when it does occur, the very foundations of the universe are shaken.)

This phantom concrete mode of expression (and the mode of experience that seems to underlie it) is one source of the traditional and widespread notion that schizophrenic-type experience is concrete in a primitive or deficient sense—a notion implying that schizophrenics, like infants or certain brain-damaged patients, are incapable of the reflective distance required for the more abstract, less stimulus-bound modes of cognition.[17] Yet it seems these reifications or concretizations may actually indicate not a lack but an exaggeration of reflective distance and self-consciousness: psychological processes and ideas the normal person would experience only tacitly or abstractly (such as kinesthetic sensations in the jaw, or the meaning of "meaning") are focused on and thereby transformed into phenomena having some of the qualities of actual physical objects existing separate from the self. Could this be what Artaud was referring to when he spoke, in a passage quoted in Chapter 2, of the tendency of his thinking to go from the "inside out" or "from the abstract to the concrete and not from the concrete toward the abstract"?

An understanding of phantom concreteness, and of the reifying, distancing, often self-alienating processes that underlie it, may help to explain why schizophrenic-type persons are so often inclined to experience and characterize their minds in physical or mechanistic terms—comparing themselves, for instance, to machines, computers, cameras, or engines of various kinds.[18] It also helps us better understand the waxing and waning of the self such individuals often describe, which need not be assumed to involve an experience of actual physical change of size, even though patients do often use a physicalistic vocabulary (speaking, e.g., of expanding and contracting like a balloon). In many instances, patients may be using concrete imagery to describe what is in essence the sort of epistemic oscillation discussed above—a shift from experiencing one's own subjectivity as an all-constituting force to experiencing it as a merely constituted entity.

The following passage from *The Umbilicus of Limbo* (1925), a work by the schizophrenic Artaud, is an especially striking example of physicalistic language being used to describe something whose nature is, in a sense, mental and inner.[19] It is also a hair-raising description of how the world catastrophe which many schizophrenics dread may be brought on by their hyperreflexivity or quasi-solipsism.

> Yes, space was yielding its whole mental padding in which no thought was yet clear or had replenished its load of objects. But little by little the mass turned like a slimy and powerful nausea, a sort of vast influx of blood, vegetal and thundering. And the rootlets which were trembling at the corners of my mind's eye detached themselves with vertiginous speed from the wind-contracted mass. And all space trembled like a vagina being pillaged by the globe of the burning sky. And something like the beak of a real dove pierced the confused mass of states, all profound thinking at this moment formed layers, resolved itself, became transparent and reduced. . . . And two or three times more the whole vegetable mass heaved, and each time my eye shifted to a more precise position. The very darkness became profuse and without object. The total frost gained clarity.[20]

Like so much of Artaud's writings (and the speech of many schizophrenics), this passage may seem difficult at first. On careful reading, however, it seems to concern a kind of epistemic oscillation between self-as-constituting-consciousness and consciousness-as-object-of-experience. Like Schreber's nerves and rays, the rootlets Artaud describes as trembling at the corners of his mind's eye symbolize his own consciousness—a consciousness that has somehow managed the impossible feat of seeing itself from *within*, as if subjectivity could perceive itself in the very act of constituting the world before it. Artaud's account is a highly atypical but nevertheless profoundly disconcerting counterexample or exception—albeit fleeting and ultimately self-destructing—to Wittgenstein's (and Schopenhauer's) point about the necessary invisibility of the eye in its visual field or of the subject in its world.

In these lines, the supposedly imperceptible epistemic or representing self—symbolized by the phantom-concrete image of rootlets of blood at the corners of Artaud's eyes—seems to flow out into its objects, become visible there, and then dissolve, a process that results in a horrifying ontological catastrophe (the vegetal mass of space trembling in response to his consciousness, as he shifts his gaze, followed by the nothingness implied by the homogeneous images of objectless darkness and total frost). The passage appears to describe what happens when the inconceivable occurs: when self-as-constituting-consciousness enters its own field as an object of awareness (while simultaneously retaining, in some fashion, its being-as-subjectivity). The normally taken-for-granted foundation or horizon of awareness is scrutinized, and this renders explicit, external, and concrete something whose very nature it is to be implicit and within. Inevitably, this process undermines, then dissolves, the normally unseen structures undergirding the possibility of a stable or meaningful experiential world.[21] And so, in this ultimate example of phantom concreteness, we have the climactic experience of the most severe schizophrenic psychosis: the world catastrophe feared by the subject who cannot forget that the world must be represented or the world will disappear.[22]

UNCANNY PARTICULARITY

In the next state to be considered, what I call "uncanny" or "mute particularity," it is the world rather than consciousness which feels transformed in some ineffable way. "The environment," says Jaspers, "is somehow different—not to a gross degree—perception is unaltered in itself but there is some change which envelops everything with a subtle, pervasive and strangely uncertain light." Whatever is perceived may seem tremendously specific and meaningful, but without the patient being able to explain why; unfamiliar events and objects may appear to be copies or repetitions of themselves. Jaspers devoted considerable attention to this supposedly incomprehensible state in which "objects and events signify something but nothing definite" and in which everything is imbued with a "distrustful, uncomfortable uncanny tension":

> A patient noticed the waiter in the coffee-house; he skipped past him so quickly and uncannily. He noticed odd behaviour in an acquaintance

> which made him feel strange; everything in the street was so different, something was bound to be happening. A passer-by gave such a penetrating glance, he could be a detective. Then there was a dog who seemed hypnotized, a kind of mechanical dog made of rubber. There were such a lot of people walking about, something must surely be starting up against the patient. All the umbrellas were rattling as if some apparatus was hidden inside them . . .
>
> The house-signs are crooked, the streets look suspicious; everything happens so quickly. The dog scratches at the door. *"I noticed particularly" is the constant remark these patients make, though they cannot say why they take such particular note of things nor what it is they suspect.* First they want to get it clear to themselves. (emphasis added)

Jaspers called this anxiety-ridden aura or state of mind the "delusional atmosphere" or "mood," adding the proviso that it is devoid of any normal emotional state (contrary to what the word "mood" might seem to imply). He downplayed the poor reality-testing aspect of delusion in favor of the mood, going so far as to argue that, if this mood is present, "a delusion may be correct in content without ceasing to be a delusion."[23]

Unlike phantom concreteness, the quality of uncanny particularity does not attach primarily to the realm of private images or sensations but to what is, from the standpoint of both observer and patient, the real or external world. For this reason, the experience is not strictly speaking either solipsistic or delusional; and one might well wonder how it relates to the concerns of this book. Actually, uncanny particularity does have close affinities with quasi-solipsism. According to Wittgenstein, who devoted much attention to an analogous vision or state of mind, this sort of mood is also bound up with the experiential stance or attitude of rigid, passive staring. And, as we shall see, it can readily lead into quasi-solipsistic experiences, as well as into delusions or so-called delusions of various other types.

In Schreber's *Memoirs*, the feeling of uncanny particularity emerges most clearly in his discussion of the wasp miracle. After describing his experience of the insects appearing in the garden, Schreber considers the commonsensical objection to his claim that these insects are purposefully created and placed before his eyes: "One will probably object that there is nothing very extraordinary in flies being about the room or wasps about in the open at certain times, etc., and that only my morbid imagination makes me believe they are divine miracles somehow related to my own person" (M, 186). Schreber possesses what seems to him to be incontrovertible proof of the impossibility of such a commonsense explanation: "I have most stringent and convincing proofs of the fact that these beings do not fly towards me by accident, but are beings newly created for my sake each time."[24] If the commonsense explanation were true, he argues, one would expect the insects to fly toward him in a random manner; if it were only a matter of his morbid imagination, the insects would appear before his eyes in arbitrary patterns and accidental sequences and numbers. It is perfectly obvious to Schreber, however, that this is not what occurs; as he insists, "These animals always appear on definite occasions and in definite order around me; . . . [therefore] they cannot possibly have existed before and only been driven into my company accidentally" (M, 186).[25] For example, when a wasp startled him while he was dozing on a bench, the event did not occur some random number of times: "This event was repeated *three times running* in my short stay," he tells us (M, 233). Schreber does not explain why three times could not itself have been an accidental number of occurrences. Nor does he explain on what definite occasions or in what kind of definite order the insects appeared. Somehow, it seems, the events just *felt* definite to him. Such a mood is fairly common in schizophrenia, especially just before or at the outbreak of a psychotic period, when patients sometimes stare intently ahead and declare that everything looks different and intensely meaningful, but without being able to say how or in what way (displaying the "truth-taking stare," as I would term this sign of encroaching schizophrenia which is characterized in German psychiatry as a stiffness or rigidity of perception—*die Wahrnehmungsstarre*).[26]

Anyone who has read the *Memoirs* will know how capable of conveying his experiences Schreber is, how articulate and forthcoming he is about even the most bizarre beliefs and behaviors. It seems highly unlikely that he is withholding some elaborate understanding of just how the insects appeared in a definite way, of just what the pattern in question was. It seems, rather, that Schreber's experience of definiteness simply could not have been described more completely: what seems to overwhelm him is just the sheer and, in a sense, abstract fact of the specificity or particularity of everything around him. It is difficult to know how to explain, or even to convey, Schreber's probable state of mind. We seem once again, as so often with schizophrenic phenomena, to be bumping our heads against the limits of our language (as Wittgenstein would say). But one thing is clear: Schreber's experience of ineffable definiteness is a central feature of his lived-world, an important element of the pervasive and uncanny mood tone that is ultimately linked with a feeling of omnipresent meaningfulness and with his own sense of being, somehow, at the center of things.

In many patients, this experience of uncanny particularity seems to be the basis for the one Schneiderian first-rank symptom of schizophrenia that does not involve extreme disturbance of ego boundaries or of the sense of volition, the symptom known as "delusional percept."[27] In delusional percept the patient has a sudden and absolutely undeniable sense that some event has a special meaning. No gross perceptual alteration is involved, no hallucination or sensory illusion. Yet, though the world looks perfectly normal, it also looks completely altered, since normal perceptual objects are now imbued with a feeling of profound meaning and absolute certainty. The patient may, for example, see a dog raising its left paw (and there really will be a dog in front of him, raising its paw), or he notices a red pickup truck parked on a bridge under which he is about to pass. At the same time, he feels absolutely sure that this is not an accidental happening, something of no significance beyond itself. It may be that the people passing by on the street assume an uncanny aspect, as if there were something too precise, too "just so" about them. Some aspect of the face or demeanor of every passer-by may seem an example or instance *of* something. Individual people may seem reminiscent of someone already known—as if, in some uncanny way, they had exactly the same nose or mouth, or exactly the same way of clutching their coat. And yet the feeling cannot be described, for there is no specific person of whom one is reminded. The feeling of familiarity, of "just-so-ness," has no reference outside itself; the passers-by are exemplary only of themselves.

The patient may rest with this inarticulable feeling of significance. Or he may feel that there is a sign in what he sees, though without being able to say what the sign means or who is its source. Finally, he may elaborate on the raw sense of significance by attributing a specific delusional meaning to it. This last development is easy enough to understand: randomness or accident does seem almost inconceivable in the presence of such a compelling sense of definiteness. To many such patients, the experience of the tremendous particularity of things and events therefore suggests that these phenomenona must be the specific way they are for some reason or because of some purposeful plan in someone's mind; the delusions that develop satisfy a yearning for such reasons or purposes (even though there may be no obvious logical connection between the perceptual phenomenon and the delusional interpretation). And so, the patient who stares at the dog or the pickup truck may actually feel a sense of epistemic relief on deciding, say, that the dog's lifting of its paw signifies that the patient is being persecuted, or that the red pickup indicates he is John the Baptist and must starve himself for forty days and forty nights.[28]

At least some of these delusions appear to make attributions concerning objects, people, or events existing within objective or consensual reality, and thus they may lack a quasi-solipsistic quality almost entirely. But uncanny particularity also generates many delusions that involve alterations in the general sense of reality, as well as delusions that seem directed toward (as if to explain or account for) the mood of pervasive particularity as a whole. Schreber, for example, concluded from the feeling of uncanny definiteness that there must be some overseeing consciousness, some pervasive intentionality that makes everything happen in just the way it does and no other (e.g., the rays or God). The particularity experience thus contributed to his sense of an externalized subjectivization, for it proved to him that what he called "spontaneous generation (parentless generation)" or "direct genesis (creation) through divine miracles" of beings—for instance, the wasp miracle—does in fact exist and "is due to the purposeful manifestations of divine power of will or divine power of creation" (M, 185, 233).

It seems clear that such delusions are dependent on or motivated by the particularity experiences that precede or underlie them. But despite this important role in the process of delusion formation, as well as in the general atmosphere and mood tone of the schizophrenic world, these subtle perceptual alterations have received little attention in the psychiatric literature.[29] Perhaps this neglect is not so surprising, given the difficulty of describing mute particularity or even of fixing it in one's mind. How, in fact, can we characterize or comprehend this experience in which everything looks so completely normal yet at the same time so indescribably, so incomprehensibly, special?

In Wittgenstein's *Brown Book* there is a long, seemingly obsessional, and at first rather mystifying sequence which seems to be a philosophical rumination on just this sort of experience. It is worth considering in some detail. As so often, Wittgenstein is concerned to criticize something in traditional philosophical thought and discourse—in this case, a certain essentializing tendency that is especially prevalent in the philosophy of mind—and he relates this to a certain experiential stance.

He begins by talking about one's propensity when philosophizing to assume that certain experiences characteristically happen in a particular way. Whenever one engages in, say, an act of reading or exercizing volition or recognizing something (e.g., recognizing the expression on someone's face, or realizing that a color seen can be characterized as red), there is a misleading temptation to assume that some characteristic experience must have occurred. The philosopher is inclined to postulate some indescribable yet definite element, perhaps some kind of enshrouding "particular atmosphere" (BBB, 167), that is supposedly definitive and partially constitutive of just that kind of experience—an element that thus constitutes the essence of, or at least is a necessary condition for, the existence of a psychological process such as reading, exercising volition, or recognizing the color red. The person who believes in the existence of this supposedly definitive and essential experience is quick to admit that it cannot, perhaps even on principle, be defined in words. Nevertheless, he typically insists, there is some quite specific phenomenon to which he is attending in his introspection about the process. If he cannot put this essence into words, he is likely to say, that just goes to show the poverty of language as a device for expressing the truth about inner experience or the mind. Such a person—Wittgenstein's imaginary interlocutor—nevertheless insists that there does exist a definite experience toward which he is gesturing, as if with the mind's nod.

Wittgenstein believes that the error underlying this way of thinking can be illuminated by considering a linguistic fact—two divergent meanings of the word "particular": "Now the use of the word 'particular' is apt to produce a kind of delusion and roughly speaking this delusion is produced by the double usage of this word" (BBB, 158). In referring to some "particular" phenomenon according to the first usage, which he calls the transitive type, one is implying that there is some way in which one could further specify the phenomenon or something to which one could compare it: the "particular" phenomenon is thus assumed to be exemplary in some way. In saying that John has a particular expression on his face, for example, one might mean that John looks angry or happy or, say, jocular-but-with-an-underlying-hint-of-sadness. (Though most of Wittgenstein's illustrative examples involve what are experienced as features of the external world, such as facial expressions or lighting in a room, his point is also meant to apply to psychological and supposedly inner processes, such as intending or recognizing.)

But one may also refer to a phenomenon as "particular" according to a second usage, which Wittgenstein calls the intransitive one. In such a case, one does not experience or remark on anything that *could* be further specified. In this experience (which we might also call mute particularity, since it involves the indescribable), one simply notices the facial expression—letting it, so to speak, sink in and make its full impression on one. Or, to take other examples, it is as if one caught one's bodily position at some random instant in the process of walking and then concentrated one's attention on just that position; or as if one decided to concentrate one's attention on the quality of light in a room (BBB, 158, 176). One is, admittedly, in *some* particular position; the room does have *some* particular lighting—but neither the position nor the light is necessarily representative of anything other than itself. Neither the face whose expression one notices nor the bodily position nor the lighting is a token of a type more general than this particular instantiation itself. In fact, Wittgenstein says, to speak of any of these as a "particular" position or expression or quality of light is a bit odd—rather like comparing something with itself. Wittgenstein sums up the two usages of "particular": "On the one hand . . . it is used preliminary to a specification, description, comparison; on the other hand, as what one might describe as an emphasis" (BBB, 158).

Wittgenstein believes, however, that there is a tendency to confuse these two types of experience, just as one might confuse the two different usages of the word "particular." There is a tendency to think, when one is having the second, intransitive, type of experience, that one is noticing the sort of thing one actually does notice in the first, transitive, type. Wittgenstein describes this mistake: "It is, when I let the face make an impression on me, as though there existed a double of its expression, as though the double was the prototype of the expression and as though seeing the expression of the face was finding the prototype to which it corresponded—as though in our mind there had been a mould and the picture we see had fallen into that mould, fitting it." (BBB, 163).

In such a moment, one engages in what Wittgenstein calls "a comparison of the object with itself, . . . a reflexive comparison" (BBB, 160). "It is," he writes elsewhere, "as if in imagination we put a thing into its own shape and saw that it fitted" (PI, §216). But this is an illusion: "We are, as it were, under an optical delusion which by some sort of reflection makes us think that there are two objects where there is only one." In actuality, "it is rather that we let the picture sink into our mind and make a mould there" (BBB, 162, 163). I may have an absolutely compelling sense of the particularity of whatever I observe; and yet, like a patient caught up in the truth-taking stare, "at the same time I am unable to point to, or get a grasp on, that 'particular way'" (BBB, 167).

As Wittgenstein analyzes it, this uncanny experience of mute particularity is one of the characteristic delusions engendered by a certain unnatural, reflective stance characteristic of philosophizing. By stepping out of the flow of life, the philosopher focuses attention on features of the world or parts of the stream of experience which, in the normal course of events, would not be separated out, fixed, and framed before the mind's eye. In contrast with the lived-world of activity and engagement, in such a state the philosopher-perceiver seems to be experiencing experience rather than the world—losing himself in contemplation of what might be called "the phenomenon of the phenomenon."[30] "I see, you're repeating to yourself some experience and again and again gazing at it," writes Wittgenstein (BBB, 165). In his view, it is the mere fact of concentrating on the experience, typically done in a state of experiential passivity and detachment, that engenders the profound impression of specificity or doubledness:

> To see this more clearly, consider another example: You are, of course, constantly changing the position of your body throughout the day; arrest yourself in any such attitude (while writing, reading, talking, etc., etc.) and say to yourself in the way in which you say "'Red' comes in a particular way . . . ", "I am now in a particular attitude." You will find that you can quite naturally say this. But aren't you always in a particular attitude? And of course you didn't mean that you were just then in a particularly striking attitude. What was it that happened? You concentrated on, as it were stared at, your sensations. And this is exactly what you did when you said that "red" came in a particular way [when you recognized a color *as* red] . . . .
>
> What is *particular* about the way "red" comes is that it comes while you're philosophizing about it, as what is particular about the position of your body when you concentrated on it was concentration. We appear to ourselves to be on the verge of describing the way, whereas we aren't really opposing it to any other way. We are emphasizing, not comparing, but we express ourselves as though this emphasis was really a comparison of the object with itself; there seems to be a reflexive comparison. (BBB, 158–60)

One feels that one is simply observing aspects or features of one's experience which, like physical objects, were already there before one chose to observe them; whereas, in fact, one is seeing experience as if "through a coloured glass." And so, by a strange paradox of the reflexive, one is unaware of the effect of one's own hyperawareness—of the fact that it is the very process of concentrated, disengaged observation that casts this weird tint of ineffable definiteness, engendering a feeling of doubledness which then seems discovered rather than invented. As Wittgenstein puts it, "By attending, looking, you produce the impression [of particularity]; you can't look at the impression." "But I don't point to the feeling by attending to it. Rather, attending to the feeling means producing or modifying it.

(On the other hand, observing a chair does not mean producing or modifying the chair.)" (BBB, 176, 174).

When this self-generating experience occurs, the world of random specifics appears in an uncanny light. That some thing should exist, or event should occur, in just *this* way and no other, suddenly seems amazing. It now seems as if the events that occur are miraculously corresponding to some predetermined and finite set of molds or forms that have a separate and prior existence, whether as preexisting events or as ideas in some purposeful consciousness. Though one is really only noticing something totally unremarkable—the fact that events do fall out in some single way at any given moment, as indeed they must—one feels as if one were observing a miraculous set of repetitions or coincidences, or the precise playing out of some definite plan. The experience may thus be bound up with a feeling of doubledness, the sheer sense that this event is in certain respects a copy of some prototype, or with a feeling of passive determinism, the feeling that everything is falling out just as it has to. One may easily be led to seek *the* meaning, intent, or cause that seems, like some Platonic or noumenal essence, to lie behind the merely phenomenal world one directly experiences:

> The same strange illusion which we are under when we seem to seek the something which a face expresses whereas, in reality, we are giving ourselves up to the features before us—that same illusion possesses us even more strongly if repeating a tune to ourselves and letting it make its full impression on us, we say "This tune says *something*", and it is as though I had to find *what* it says. And yet I know that it doesn't say anything such that I might express in words or pictures what it says. And if, recognizing this, I resign myself to saying "It just expresses a musical thought", this would mean no more than saying "It expresses itself". (BBB, 166)

However, continues Wittgenstein, "the idea suggests itself that there *must* be a paradigm somewhere in our mind," a specific and potentially specifiable paradigm to which the tune conforms.

The symbols experienced in such moments are, at the same time, charged with a sense of meaning yet empty of any specific or describable meaning; one might call them "symbol symbols"—symbolic vehicles whose only real referent is that most general phenomenon, the tantalizing presence of meaning itself. One effect of this experience (not described in quite this way by Wittgenstein) is to downplay the sense of the authentic existence, the brute thereness or being of the thing perceived, in favor of the sense of essence. For essence, we might say, precedes existence in the queasy reality of this ontologically insecure and paranoid form of life; the sense of some undefined yet definable essence is always pointing away from what is present toward some elusive, hidden, and seemingly more authentic meaning that lies elsewhere.[31]

As we see, then, the sheer quality of definiteness may prevent one from feeling that anything one notices could be the way it is merely by chance. One possible consequence is that, instead of simply accepting things as they are, the person becomes obsessed with the question, Why? Such a person may thus lapse into what, in Wittgenstein's view, is a misplaced and endless yearning for explanations or definitions when, in fact, careful descriptions are all that is truly appropriate. This is a common philosophical and intellectual disease, the failure to realize that at a certain point one reaches bedrock and should "turn one's spade" (in the famous image from the *Investigations*, §217):

> Why do you demand explanations? If they are given you, you will once more be facing a terminus. They cannot get you any further than you are at present.
>
> . . . the solution of the difficulty is a description, if we give it the right place in our considerations. If we dwell upon it, and do not try to get beyond it.
>
> The difficulty here is: to stop. (Z,58, §315, §314)

Wittgenstein considered Freudian thought to be a prime example of this self-generating, self-perpetuating mania for explanation; another instance is the philosopher's relentless pursuit of hidden essences—of the essence of language or the proposition, of exercising volition or seeing red. A philosophy more truly "therapeutic," such as Wittgenstein's own approach was intended to be, must by contrast refuse to "advance any kind of theory [or] anything hypothetical"; it must "do away with all *explanation*, and description alone must take its place" (PI, §109).

In Wittgenstein's view, the futile questioning characteristic of philosophers tends to arise from some hitch in, or withdrawal from, the normal context and flow of existence. It is less likely to afflict someone who engages in practical activity rather than withdrawing into passive contemplation, someone who uses language in an everyday rather than a philosophical or metaphysical fashion. Not surprisingly, Wittgenstein's own relationship to these issues was complicated and full of ambivalence; though in one sense an antiphilosopher, a critic of the illusions born of philosophical abstraction and detachment, he also had much in common with the philosophers he criticized. Not only did he concern himself with their problems and questions (even if only to deny them); his way of resolving or dissolving these problems also depended on withdrawal, in his case, in fact, on a double withdrawal, a standing-back not merely from the speech of the marketplace but from the normal philosophical conversation as well. It is understandable, therefore, that Wittgenstein's oft-expressed desire that "philosophical problems should *completely* disappear" was also a wish to be relieved of his own antiphilosophical tendencies. "The real discovery," as he put it in the *Investigations*, "is the one that makes me capable of stopping doing philosophy when I want to. —The one that gives philosophy peace, so that it is no longer tormented by questions which bring *itself* in question" (PI, §133). But this philosophical affliction was not easily evaded, it seems, despite the efforts of his antiphilosophizing: as he once put it to his friend M. O'C. Drury, "You know I said I can stop doing philosophy when I like. That is a lie! I *can't*."[32]

The various feelings we have been considering in this section—feelings of uncanny definiteness, doubledness, and determinism, of ineffable meanings lying just beyond reach—are certainly frequent among schizophrenics. The reader will recall Jaspers's description of those patients whose worlds bristled with a disconcerting sense of significance, who were constantly saying "I noticed particularly" without being able to explain themselves further. Eugen Bleuler describes a patient for whom the sense of doubledness manifested itself in a pervasive sense of déjà vu: "For a long period of time, one of our hebephrenics believed that he had experienced exactly one year before everything that was happening. The very same visitor in exactly the same clothes was here one year ago today and said the same things." A different patient felt that he had made up the story he had just read and had even told it to his brother long ago. Another patient, at the Burghölzli hospital, expressed his feelings of particularity and inauthenticity through his belief that what he saw was a kind of second world. He claimed he was now confined in an identical Russian Burghölzli that had been erected as an exact copy of Bleuler's asylum in Switzerland.[33]

The doubledness experience can also occur in conjunction with a sense of predestination or purpose. To the patient, everything may seem to have been foretold, either by other people or, perhaps more commonly, by the patient. "I seem to have lived all the events I have read about or heard about or knew by heart," said one schizophrenic.[34] Schreber at times had the feeling that everyone he knew was someone from his earlier life. I have already mentioned a related manifestation of mute particularity in his world: his feeling of being surrounded by "miracled-up" pseudo-beings, whose particular way of appearing—always in a definite order—showed they were "purposeful manifestations of divine power of will or divine power of creation" (M, 185).

Schreber's sense of particularity also made him succumb to the obsessive asking of the question Why and to a relentless kind of doubting, tendencies that are criticized by Wittgenstein. In one remarkable passage in the *Memoirs*, in fact, Schreber describes being overcome by a veritable mania for explanation in which he was forced "to ponder many things usually passed over by human beings" (M, 179)—to wonder about the "reason or purpose" that accounted for why things were just as they were:

> I meet a person I know by the name of Schneider. Seeing him the thought arises "This man's name is Schneider" or "This is Mr. Schneider." With it "But why" or "Why because" also resounds in my nerves. . . . This very peculiar question 'why' occupies my nerves automatically. . . . My nerves perhaps answer first: Well, the man's name is Schneider because his father was also called Schneider. But this trivial answer does not really pacify my nerves. Another chain of thought starts about why giving of names was introduced at all among people, its various forms among dif-

> ferent peoples at different times, and the various circumstances . . . which gave rise to them. (M, 180)

Schreber's attitude toward this "compulsive thinking"—which, he said, "throw[s] into my nerves unconnected conjunctions expressing causal or other relations ('Why only', 'Why because', 'Why because I' . . .)"—was deeply ambivalent. He writes, in one passage, that "being continually forced to trace the causal relation of every happening, every feeling, and every idea has given me gradually deeper insight into the essence of almost all natural phenomena and aspects of human activity in art, science, etc., than is achieved by people who do not think it worth while to think about ordinary everyday occurrences" (M, 179). But Schreber also had an almost Wittgensteinian sense of the absurdity and futility of this constant questioning. Of his own speculations about Schneider, he writes, "In ordinary human contact the answer would probably be: 'Why! What a silly question, the man's name is simply Schneider.' But my nerves were unable or almost unable to behave like this" (M, 180). "Indeed most often the question why is inept," he writes, "as for instance in such sentences as 'This rose has a nice smell' or 'This poem has a beautiful poetical expression' or 'This is a magnificent painting.' . . . Nevertheless this question is stimulated in me by the voices and moves me to think" (M, 179). Furthermore, Schreber seems to have recognized that this kind of excessive reflection could lead to paralyzing doubt and indecision, as is clear in the following passage: "The 'thinking-it-over-thought' denoted something perhaps also known to psychologists: it often leads a person to turn his will power in the opposite direction or at least change it from that which at first he may have felt inclined to follow, but which on further consideration *automatically causes doubts*" (M, 141).

It seems, then, that (as Schreber himself came to recognize) he often labored under an illusion, the same illusion Wittgenstein so often criticized in philosophers: the assumption that there must be a reason for everything; that, since nothing happens without a cause (or without the playing out of some underlying and hidden essence), seeking explanations is always valid and worthwhile. In fact, according to Wittgenstein, no possible answer can provide an escape from such relentless and futile questioning, which "keeps the mind pressing against a blank wall, thereby preventing it from ever finding the outlet." "To show a man how to get out you have first of all to free him from the misleading influence of the question" (BBB, 169). One needs to show, for example, that when doubting affects everything, doubt itself "gradually loses its sense"—since doubting is in fact ultimately dependent on "non-doubting behaviour" (OC, §56, §354).

To unmask a temptation, thus destroying its appeal: this is the core of Wittgenstein's method, and this is precisely what he was trying to do with his discussions of doubt and certainty as well as with his analyses of the linguistic delusion inherent in the word "particular" and the (closely related) "optical" delusion engendered by staring too intently at the circumstances before one's eyes.

It is not easy to find evocative autobiographical descriptions of the experience of mute particularity in its purest form. The mood is both ineffable and unstable; it readily flees into other experiential states that seem to account for it or place it in some way—such as delusions of conspiracy or determinism and feelings of déjà vu. One schizophrenic mentioned earlier, the patient who compared himself to a Xerox machine, seems to have had such experiences, and his (admittedly rather ambiguous) description is worth considering in this light. He told me how, during a catatonic phase of his illness, he had been looking at the birds outside his window and had suddenly felt overwhelmed by how "paramount" and "perfect" everything was. It was clear that he was not making a conventional remark about the beauty of the birds' plumage or biological form. Rather, it was as if, to him, their every motion was "just so"—this bird seeming to light on a branch in just this way, that one swooping in a certain arc, not at a random moment but at this particular instant of time. When I asked what he meant by "paramount" and "perfect," he did not know what to say at first, but he then ventured, rather uncertainly, that it had felt to him as if the birds were "determined." Pressing him further, I asked how they were determined, by whom or by what, but he only looked perplexed and finally replied that it must be by "the people who know about birds."

One cannot be entirely certain of the meaning of such remarks. They do suggest, however, that for this patient mute particularity was associated with a sense of determinism, and this with a feeling that the world was somehow pervaded by "knowing." I would argue that this sense of pervasive knowing might have been, in essence, a manifestation of his own hyperreflexive concentration; that this is what gave him the feeling of the birds being twice-seen, and thus as seeming to coincide miraculously with their own being in such a paramount and perfect way. Given this interpretation, the "people who know about birds" would be none other than the patient—an externalization of himself, looking. In watching the birds, he did not feel in the presence of a shared or objective world; rather, he was in a sense experiencing his own experience and finding that it coincided with itself. This feeling of a felt subjectivization that is nevertheless alien ("the people who know about birds") recalls the examples of quasi-solipsism considered earlier in the discussion of solipsistic loss of self.

A literary expression of a similar experience occurs in Robert Musil's novella "The Perfecting of a Love," in which the woman protagonist speaks of a feeling she had several nights before, at a moment when she suddenly felt estranged and alone and the world stood forth in a new light that shattered her sense of communion with her husband:

> "Do you remember," the woman suddenly said, "a few nights ago, when you held me in your arms—? Did you realise there was something between us then? . . . it wasn't anything *real*, I was really close to you, and all the same it was there like a vague shadow, it was as if I could be far from you and could exist without you. Do you know that feeling—how sometimes everything is suddenly there twice over, one sees all the things around one, complete and distinct as one has known them all along, and then once again, pale, twilit, and aghast, as if they were already being regarded, stealthily and with an alien gaze, by someone else? I wanted to take you and wrench you back into myself—and then again to push you away and fling myself on the ground because it could happen at all.[35]

It is significant that such experiences generally happen at moments when the person feels isolated and is inactive or otherwise in a passive stance. The patient's sense of the perfectness of the birds, for instance, occurred during a semicatatonic period when he mostly lay in bed or occasionally staggered, zombielike, around the hospital ward. Another patient I treated, at a time when everything looked uncannily different to him and he exhibited the truth-taking stare, maintained that he would never have "gone crazy" if he had not made the mistake, one night at a party just before his psychotic break, of sitting back on the couch and watching the goings-on instead of joining in. There is, of course, much more to a psychotic break than this. Nevertheless, it is significant that schizophrenic patients often do report that performing some action or interacting with others makes their odd perceptual experiences disappear—that when they comb their hair or shovel snow, for instance, the world turns normal again, at least for a time.[36]

PRIMITIVITY, MODERNISM, AND THE UNCANNY

Most psychoanalysts who have addressed themselves to the uncanny, anxiety-laden moods so common in early schizophrenia have, predictably enough, interpreted them as manifestations of regression, or of premonitions of regression, to early stages of cognitive and psychosexual development. The analyst Marguerite Sechehaye, for example, writes that her patient Renée's early feelings of estrangement, which involved such experiences of uncanny definiteness, heralded the "deep regression" of her ego "to the earliest evolutionary phases" or the "fetal level." The psychiatrist Silvano Arieti expresses a similar view in his influential book on schizophrenia. He sees the pervasively anxious mood that often precedes a psychotic break as a response to the reactivation of "primary process mechanisms and their original contents." The mood is a reaction to revivals of traumatic memories of infancy and early childhood that had previously been repressed, memories involving a horrendous sense of threat to the feeling of self-worth, and to the reemergence of archaic forms of thinking by which these traumatic memories come to be elaborated and magnified.[37]

This view is close to Freud's own explanation of what he calls the "uncanny," a form of experience that would seem to include the schizoid or schizophrenic mood state of mute particularity. Freud defines the uncanny as "that class of the terrifying which leads back to something long known to us, once very familiar." In his view it always involves an actual remembering of some early experience that has been repressed—a remembering which, however, is not recognized *as* a remembering by the individual having the experience. What is evoked or reactivated can be threatening mental contents in the form of repressed complexes or else primitive modes or forms of thought of "a very early mental stage" (such as the infantile experience of self-world fusion or the omnipotence of thought).[38]

Both the lived-world of mute particularity and that of infancy are, of course, very different from normal, pragmatic adult consciousness; in this purely negative sense they have something in common—a shared difference from. But if one takes a careful look at the phenomenology of these schizophrenic experiences, they seem in many respects quite antithetical to infantile states. According to virtually all developmental theories, including those of the psychoanalytic schools, the world of the infant and young child is pervaded by an intense and dynamic sense of emotional involvement. Even inanimate objects and space itself are perceived largely in terms of their affective resonance for the perceiving child. Further, the world of the infant is not yet felt to be a thing wholly separate from the self, for there prevails a quasi-mystical sense of union between subject and object.

The schizophrenic experiences I have discussed here could hardly be more different: as we have seen, they involve not mystic union and emotional involvement but a profound disengagement from reality and detachment from the processes of life. Indeed, the schizophrenic "delusional mood" is, in a sense, not a mood at all: normal emotionality is replaced by a characteristic anxiety and a hyperaware, purely cognitive sense of meaningfulness. What might serve as a more apt analogy than infancy, it seems to me, is the alienated vision of certain modernist and postmodernist artists, many of whom seem to have taken to heart the protosurrealist painter Giorgio de Chirico's famous admonition "to live in the world as if in a vast museum of strangeness."[39] The literary scholar Erich Kahler has described the uncanny magic of many central examples of twentieth-century art as manifesting a certain "schizesthesia," an "insistent, overstressed correctness" or "lucid indifference" so devoid of normal emotional resonance as to result in a "disjunction of the organic, disjunction of the sensorially coherent being, of the person and of the object." Though Kahler calls this "a new mysticism" in modernist art, it is perhaps better described as an antimysticism—involving not an embracing of all things and of self and world into a single unity but the opposite, fragmentation and estrangement. It is significant that Kahler should describe these developments as signs not of regression but of progression, cruel consequences of the "steady growth of man's self-reflection and psychological introspection" and of a "mental microscopy" that turns on both self and world. Though in one sense this attitude represents the triumph of consciousness and volitional control, it is in another sense the opposite: thus, it happens like a compulsion, and "the man who looks seems himself to be just an instrument, or victim, of this irresistible seeing."[40]

The novel *Nadja* by André Breton, the high priest of surrealism, is one of the clearest expressions of this sensibility. Breton describes his wanderings around Paris in a state of disengaged contemplation, making himself an "agonized witness" before whose gaze loom up quintessentially surrealist experiences of mute particularity: "facts which may belong to the order of pure observation, but which on each occasion present all the appearance of a signal, without our being able to say precisely which signal." Though the author-protagonist is not literally inactive in *Nadja*, he is experientially so—moving about Paris as a sort of meandering passivity who takes the world as spectacle rather than as a field of action or involvement.[41]

For a more vivid sense of what it may be like to experience the "delusional mood," it is worth dwelling for a moment on a more recent exemplar of this alienated sensibility, one that could be said to take mute particularity as its central theme: the photography of Diane Arbus. Arbus's photographs nearly always capture some weird exemplariness about the people they show, yet this quality is always something one cannot pinpoint: thus, her people are never types, yet they *are* types. "There are always two things that happen," Arbus wrote in her notebooks. "One is recognition and the other is that it's totally peculiar."[42] The subtlest and in my opinion most disconcerting of her photographs are not the ones depicting the literally freakish—retarded people, midgets, giants—but those of relatively normal individuals. In these works it is more evident that the feeling of strangeness or peculiarity comes not from the object shown so much as from the perspective or attitude adopted, an attitude that evokes a disconcertingly intransitive kind of particularity.

The classic Arbus photograph in this regard is reproduced on the cover of her well-known collection. There is something undeniably grotesque about these twin, dark-haired girls who stand at attention and stare dutifully into the camera, yet if one looks at either sister, her face and body seem normal enough. Only after a while does one realize that it is their very similarity to each other that is grotesque—as if the ineffable and surreal exemplariness of each, usually a psychological *impression* (and one that, in other Arbus photographs, one is likely to have about a single individual), had been embodied and now stood there, mockingly and in the flesh, at each girl's side. The viewer's eye moves back and forth between the images as if seeking to discover which twin is the realer and more perfect one and which the imitation. But the more one looks at the face of either girl, the more her face is likely to seem ineffably particular, like a version of something other and realer than itself to which it seems, somehow, to allude. As one's gaze moves to the other twin, however, the same thing happens again; now this one seems to be a copy of the other. The similarity always leaves one with the sense that *this* reality, the one being contemplated now, is both flawed and secondary—that the true reality resides elsewhere. Being seems to recede, as if overwhelmed by a tantalizing, never quite present or graspable meaning. It is as if the actual doubledness of the twin girls were objectifying the doubled vision of uncanny particularity—with its "mould and the picture we see [that has] fallen into that mould, fitting it" (BBB,163). This futile and endless shifting epitomizes intransitive particularity—an experience which, as Wittgenstein implies with his many metaphors of futility, seems constantly to be pointing somewhere beyond itself when, all the while, it is only circling back on its own ineffable essence.[43]

AN APOLLONIAN ILLNESS

In psychoanalysis, delusions are typically understood as manifesting one or both of two factors: especially intense, unneutralized emotions or desires (an unruly id), and a weakened capacity for control of these desires or for maintaining accurate awareness of, and separation from, external reality (a weak ego or weak ego boundaries). Wherever one puts the emphasis, the presence of delusions is likely to imply the ascendancy of impulse or affect over consciousness, of id over the ego. But, as we have seen, schizoid and schizophrenic lived-worlds often involve something rather different: not an overwhelming by but detachment from the instinctual sources of vitality, not immersion in the sensory surround but disengagement from a derealized external world, not stuporous waning of awareness but hypertrophy of consciousness and the conceptual life. One psychoanalyst has interpreted the schizoids and schizophrenic's preoccupation with the inner world and their own mental life as "a libidinization of the thought processes";[44] to me it seems more apt to speak of a cerebralization of instinct and the body.

It is significant, then, that many schizophrenic patients describe the world of psychosis as a place not of darkness but of relentless light—light being the natural metaphor for conscious awareness. The schizophrenic patient Renée speaks of the insane as "enlightened people"; to become mad is, for her, not to descend into the depths or the darkness but to enter the "Land of Enlightenment"—which is also the "Land of Unreality." Her description of this realm of Unreality evokes the lucidity and surreal precision of an Arbus photograph or a de Chirico painting: "a country, opposed to Reality, where reigned an implacable light, blinding, leaving no place for shadow."[45] Similarly, in describing his "nervous illness," Schreber speaks of his head and body as being "illuminated by rays" (M, 117n), rays that can be read as manifestations of his own self-conscious awareness. It is also significant that the schizophrenic-type world so closely fits the description of solipsism—the illusory doctrine which, for Wittgenstein, is the quintessential example of the philosophical illness, that tendency to overvalue and reify abstract, contemplative thought and to lose contact with the true sources of wisdom that are to be found in a life of engagement and activity. Wittgenstein understood very well the potential of a certain kind of mind to drive itself mad through its own relentless lucidity. The analogies with solipsism suggest that schizophrenia may be less a Dionysian than an Apollonian, or perhaps a Socratic, illness: a matter of the mind's perverse triumph over the body, the emotions, and the external world.

CONCLUSION

So far this book has been fairly limited in scope. I have not even touched on questions concerning the origins of Schreber's way of being—on issues raised by biological, psychodynamic, and family-systems hypotheses, for example; even my phenomenological reading has treated only certain formal or structural features of his lived-world.[1] In concluding I shall not attempt a comprehensive interpretation of the Schreber case in all its aspects; but I would like to contrast my interpretation of Schreber with those of previous writers, to consider some implications of my approach for a general understanding of Schreber's symptomatology, and, in passing, to offer a few last remarks on Wittgenstein's attitudes toward philosophy and life.

Freud offers sexuality, homosexuality in particular, as the fundamental explanatory factor in Schreber's psychosis. He sees Schreber's paranoid delusions as a compromise formation, a double transformation that both expresses and disguises an underlying homosexual fantasy rooted in a preoedipal psychosexual fixation. Since "I (a male) desire him" is too threatening a wish for the conscious ego to abide, this wish is first reversed, then projected. "I desire him" becomes "I hate him," which in turn becomes "he hates me." Later psychoanalytic writers, such as Harold Searles and Robert White, have preferred to emphasize oral-stage psychosexuality and the role of primitive fantasies concerning the mother.[2] According to all these psychoanalytic views, the key to the Schreberian cosmos, and to other similar paranoid systems, lies in the dynamics of instinctual desire.

The major revisionist readings of the Schreber case have emphasized not sexuality but power. Elias Canetti, for example, ends his monumental *Crowds and Power* with a political interpretation of the Schreberian cosmos as the ultimate expression of lust for control over others—in fact, as a private premonition of the tyrannical and totalitarian fantasies soon to be unleashed in the Germany of the Third Reich.[3] Other variants of the power interpretation have been offered by William Niederland and by Morton Schatzman, a psychoanalyst and a psychiatrist who emphasize the authoritarian child-rearing methods of Schreber's father, an influential pedagogue in late-nineteenth century Germany. Each of them reads Schreber's delusions as the enduring imprint of the father's oppressive and intrusive child-rearing practices, which were intended to root out and suppress much of the child's natural spontaneity, willfulness, and independence. In contrast with Canetti's more phenomenological reading, which stresses fantasies of possessing power and grandeur, these authors, who are more interested in the life-historical roots, emphasize the delusions of being subordinated and controlled. But for them, as for Canetti, the sexual themes—such as being transformed into a woman—are at the deepest level expressions less of libidinal wishes than of power relationships.[4]

I do not wish to deny that these interpetations may offer some valid insights. No doubt, each contains a significant measure of truth that ought to be included in that nearly infinite task, a comprehensive reading of the Schreber case. I suggest, however, that these approaches are in important respects incomplete and superficial.[5] In my view, to grasp the distinctive meaning of sex and power in the Schreberian cosmos—and in the worlds of many schizoids and schizophrenics—one must first understand a dimension that is more fundamental for such individuals, that of knowledge. Let us, then, consider power and sexuality in the light of the essentially epistemological themes of Schreber's quasi-solipsism.

Schreber's paranoid preoccupations, his so-called delusions concerning the issues of controlling and being controlled, have a distinctively mental flavor; they seem less political than epistemological in nature. His grandiose delusions, for example, do not emphasize fantasies of dominion over hordes of others—like images of endless armies, say, passing in lockstep before his review. Unlike the schizophrenic imagined in the Büchner play ("Generalissimo Grasshopper, assemble the troops; Lord Spider, my Minister of Finance, I need more money"), the issue for Schreber is not who commands the world but who knows, and thus constitutes, it. What he began to fear at the onset of his illness was not that someone was trying to control his behavior but that there was a conspiracy to "destroy his reason" (M, 211–12), his capacity to be a conscious center. God wanted to commit "soul-murder" by influencing his nervous system and "imprisoning his will power" (M, 35), and by "representing" him in various ways. Later he became concerned that God did not want to admit, or perhaps did not realize, that there were other conscious centers in the universe and therefore was treating him as an inanimate thing. Indeed, he writes, there arose from God "the almost monstrous demand that I should behave continually as if I myself were a corpse" (M, 127). In his grandiose moments, Schreber reverses this epistemological relationship, now referring to himself as "the greatest seer of spirits [*Geisterseher*] of all centuries," indeed, "of all *millennia*" (M, 88). All these imaginings seem to express the fears and fantasies of the solipsist: will I turn out to be the magnificently unique conscious center of the All, or only some nonconscious object, perhaps a mere figment in the eye of some other mind?

Canetti has pointed out that Schreber's fantasies of power are reminiscent of those of a tribal shaman, yet more total. Whereas the shaman wants simply to control the spirits that flit about in the night, Schreber's dream is that spirits should be drawn down toward himself and perish therein.[6] For example, he sometimes hears the spirit of his wife saying (more precisely, he hears it "represented as saying") "let me . . . "—words he knew to mean let me "dissolve in my husband's body" (M, 116n). Since the spirits of Schreber's cosmos represent potentially rivalrous conscious centers, their perishing in him can be interpreted as a conceding of defeat in the competition of consciousnesses. If this is a power fantasy, then surely it is an epistemological one: the spectacle of other consciousnesses acceding to one's own wish to stand as the universe's only conscious center. So we can understand why Schreber's ultimate fantasy of power was not to be the most powerful man but to be the only human being left alive. And, as we know, he actually felt at times that this solipsistic fantasy had come true, that all those around him were but "hastily-improvised men" devoid of consciousness while he himself was a godlike consciousness or, at the very least, the sole conduit to, the only sense organ of, such a constituting center—a center that Schreber refers to in one passage as "a controlling sun, of which our astronomy knows nothing" (M, 95n).

Canetti interprets the fantasy of being the only one left alive as but the logical conclusion of the desire for total power. This may be so. But, if such is the case, the power fantasy must have crossed into a realm quite different from what the term "power" usually connotes. In this kind of universe, the very separateness of the world, the inertia of things and the potential opposition of rivals, has disappeared, along with any need to express power through action. Indeed, total *in*activity comes to be the very foundation of this peculiarly epistemological and passive form of power. The struggle to achieve such a condition of centrality or preeminence is purely mental—a competition of consciousnesses, so to speak. For many schizophrenics, the very fact of looking at someone or being seen by them comes to be experienced as a sort of ultimate, ontological battle—a fight to determine whose thoughts will be in the active role of controlling, constituting subject and whose will play the role of the passive object that is controlled and constituted. The issue, in the vocabulary of one schizophrenic's delusional system, is whether one is to be an "operator" or a "thing."[7]

It is not just power that has a distinctively epistemological cast in Schreber's world. I would contend that even sexuality—the realm treated by classical Freudians as the ultimate grounding of meaning, the referent of all referents—must in this case also be understood in the context of the epistemological yearnings and anxieties inherent in the solipsistic competition of consciousnesses. To understand this, it is necessary to see how, in the Schreberian cosmos, masculine and feminine identitities are associated with the fundamental epistemological and ontological modes of being—mind and body, subjecthood and objecthood.

It is clear in the *Memoirs* that Schreber experiences God's rays, the "operators" that constitute the world, as having a masculine nature, whereas the "things" known *by* God's consciousness tend to be feminine: Schreber tells us, for example, that "everything feminine attracts God's nerves." As has often been pointed out, most famously in Simone de Beauvoir's *The Second Sex,* this is a fairly standard association in Western culture. At least since the Greeks, nature and the body have been associated with the feminine, culture and the mind with the masculine. Even the metaphors embedded in our language and thought imply that the role of the male is to act and to know, the female to be acted upon and known. Schreber follows this pattern closely, even implying, in his peculiar, quasi-metaphorical fashion, that simply occupying the role of epistemological object can transform one into a female being. Thus, he writes of "the tendency innate in the Order of the World, according to which a human being ('a seer of spirits') must under certain circumstances be 'unmanned' (transformed into a woman) once he has entered into indissoluble contact with divine nerves (rays)" (M, 69).

The very quality of attracting attention, of being object rather than subject of consciousness, seems necessarily to imply femininity for Schreber. "When the rays approach, my breast gives the impression of a pretty well-developed female bosom," he writes (M, 207); but when God's constituting consciousness recedes, there is a lessening of these female qualities. In passages like the following, God's rays and Schreber's body seem to play out a sort of epistemological minuet, the partners only becoming what they are—masculine or feminine, subject or object—in their approach to and separation from each other:

> I have to add that the female characteristics which are developing on my body show a certain periodicity at increasingly shorter intervals. The reason is that everything feminine attracts God's nerves. Hence as often as one wishes to withdraw from me, one attempts to make the female characteristics which are evident on my body recede by miracle; the effect is that the structures which I call "nerves of voluptuousness" are pushed a little under the surface, that is to say are not so distinctly palpable on the

> skin, my bosom becomes a little flatter, etc. But when after a short time the rays have to approach again, the "nerves of voluptuousness" (to retain this term) become more marked, my bosom bulges again, etc. Such changes occur at present in as short a period as a few minutes. (M, 206)

In these acts of seeing-as, the feminine aspect waxes and wanes predictably, in accordance with the shifting of epistemological role and in perfect coordination with Western conceptions of gender, which are summed up in the following lines from John Berger: "Men act and women appear. Men look at women. Women watch themselves being looked at. . . . The surveyor of woman in herself is male; the surveyed female. Thus she turns herself into an object—and most particularly an object of vision: a sight."[8] One passage from the *Memoirs* suggests that Schreber has a rather explicit awareness of the role of women as object of the gaze:

> Further, the souls knew that male voluptuousness is stimulated by the sight of female nudes, but on the contrary female voluptuousness to a very much lesser extent if at all by the sight of male nudes, while female nudes stimulate *both* sexes equally. . . . I do not know whether these phenomena are generally known and considered correct. My own observations and the behaviour of my own nerves of voluptuousness leave me in no doubt that the soul-conception is correct in this respect. (M, 142)

It is clear, in any case, that Schreber's profoundly ambivalent feelings about being transformed into a woman cannot be adequately understood apart from these epistemological relations. For Schreber, transformation into a woman implies losing in the competition of consciousnesses, ceding one's epistemological centrality and becoming a mere object defined by the other's sovereign awareness. At times he experiences this sexual transformation as something monstrous, shameful, even annihilating: "unmanning" and "soul murder" are synonymous terms for him. Yet, clearly, he is also *drawn* to this transmutation into objecthood. To understand how this can be so, we must recall the negative side of solipsism and related forms of identification with the mind.

We have seen that even the achievement of the sense of absolute epistemological centrality cannot bring total serenity. The quasi-solipsist world is necessarily poisoned by a "strangely uncertain light":[9] along with a sense of power and centrality go feelings of anxiety, queasiness, and frightening responsibility—feelings of anxious particularity, of devitalization, and of the ontological flimsiness of the All. Further, as we saw in Chapter 2, the sense of self is afflicted by an inescapable paradox, undermined by the very solipsistic impulse that might be expected to aggrandize it. Finally, separation from the lived body—or transmutation of it into body-as-idea—cuts one off from the major source not only of pain and pleasure but of the sentiment of being that perhaps is pleasure's true meaning. Body as external substance or as idea, mere figment in a mental universe, can hardly provide much sense of vitality or ontological grounding. It should not be surprising, then, to find powerful counterforces at work in a solipsistic lifeworld—urges toward physicality rather than Being-as-Consciousness, or toward forms of absorbed engagement that might blot out the mind.

Wittgenstein, it seems, was very familiar with both sides of this dilemma. Though drawn as a young man toward schizoid and solipsistic ideals—the vision of an inner self completely separate from the body, and of an experiential self, the "philosophical I," fully conscious of its independence of others and the world ("What has history to do with me? Mine is the first and only world!" he wrote in his wartime notebooks in 1916; NB, 82)—Wittgenstein became, with age, far more sensitive to the feelings of vacuity, devitalization, and isolation to which such separation or retreat could lead; in 1931 he laments having "to appear like an empty tube which is simply inflated by a mind." This discontentment sometimes extended to the whole of philosophy and the intellectual life. "Wisdom is grey," he wrote in 1947. "Life on the other hand and religion are full of colour." Whereas faith is "a passion," "wisdom is cold and to that extent stupid"; it "merely *conceals* life from you . . . like cold grey ash, covering up the glowing embers" (CV, 11, 62, 56).

In his ambivalence regarding philosophizing, which he described as a source of "deep disquietudes" but also of "vague mental uneasiness" and "mental cramps," even "torments" (PI, §111, §133; L,27),[10] Wittgenstein was invoking an ancient dilemma, one to which Schreber seems also to have been heir: the question of whether thinking should be considered the truest expression or the most profound negation of the human condition. Wittgenstein in his later work was usually closer to the second, more negative view—attacking the intellectualism of the Western philosophical tradition and seeking to root human existence in the exigencies of practical and social life, even, at times, in the most creaturely, instinctual part of human nature: "I want to regard man here as an animal," he wrote just a few weeks before his death, "as a primitive being to which one grants instinct but not ratiocination. As a creature in a primitive state. . . . Language did not emerge from some kind of ratiocination" (OC, 62).

Schreber's ambivalence about the life of the mind was equally strong, but played out on a rather more excruciating, literal, and at times bizarre plane. He is proud to be "the greatest seer . . . of all centuries," and believes that nothing more terrible could befall a person such as himself than to lose or fail to exercise the capacity for reason (M, 88, 212).[11] To stop thinking, even for a moment, is to seem—perhaps to become—demented; to lose self-awareness is to be reduced to the level of a plant or a corpse (M, 153, 166, 198, 192–93, 48–49). "On the other hand," Schreber points out, "continual thinking, uninterrupted activity of the *nerves of intellect* without any respite, such as the rays impose on me through compulsive thinking, is equally incompatible with human nature." He goes so far as to describe his compulsive thinking as "mental torture"—a state one might picture by imagining "the rays of a whole world—somehow mechanically fastened at their point of issue—which travel around one single head and attempt to tear it asunder and pull it apart in a fashion comparable to quartering" (M, 123n, 136).

Schreber is very clear about the essential incompatibility between his almost constant need to be mentally aware and any normal feeling of serenity, especially physical serenity: "Every mental activity," he writes, "is always accompanied by a considerable decrease in bodily well-being" (M, 210). When directed toward the body, his characteristically intense, self-scrutinizing awareness makes him focally aware of normally implicit bodily sensations and images, which tend now to be experienced as a kind of psychosomatic discomfort: "All manner of painful states occur alternately (namely whenever God withdraws again), almost without exception quite suddenly and vanishing equally regularly after a short time . . . sciatica, cramp in the calves, states of paralysis, sudden attacks of hunger, and suchlike . . . lumbago and toothache . . . almost uninterrupted headaches of a kind certainly unknown to other human beings" (M, 201). It is noteworthy that these occur only when God withdraws, that is, when a condition of divided, self-monitoring awareness is set up. This is particularly evident in the case of the headaches, which Schreber describes as "tearing and pulling pains . . . caused by the attempt of rays [which stand for the self-monitoring part of the mind], tied-to-celestial-bodies, to withdraw from me when soul-voluptuousness [which involves the merging or near-merging of nerves and rays] has become very strong" (M, 201).[12] In reaction, Schreber developed methods to desist from what he called "compulsive thinking" and to rest his self-conscious "nerves of intellect." Perhaps the most important of these, alluded to in the passage just quoted, involves the pursuit of physical pleasure, something he strongly associates with femininity.[13] The experience of feminization was, in fact, Schreber's major antidote to the intellect, his palliative for the self-torturing mind. Though on one level a sign of persecution and defeat, it also had soothing and reassuring effects, allaying the restlessness and insidious self-undermining brought on by his compulsive thinking and self-consciousness.

Schreber believed that "the feeling of sensual pleasure—whatever its physiological basis—occurs in the female to a higher degree than in the male, involves the whole body, and . . . the mammae particularly play a very large part" (M, 205). It was particularly the passive experience of pleasure that Schreber equated with femininity. To make himself feel feminine, he needed only to stroke himself—or, rather, to *be* stroked, for in these moments he felt identified not with his active (masculine) hand but with the passive (feminine) flesh that was touched. In this way he felt (and, in a sense, brought into existence) the female "nerves of voluptuousness" that he believed to be especially numerous beneath the skin of women:

> For myself I am *subjectively certain* that my body—as I have repeatedly stated in consequence of divine miracles—shows such organs to an extent as only occurs in the female body. When I exert light pressure with my hand on any part of my body I can *feel* certain string or cord-like structures under the skin. . . . Through pressure on one such structure I

> can produce a feeling of female sensuous pleasure, particularly if I think of something feminine. (M, 205)[14]

But, Schreber insists, "I do this, by the way, not for sensual lust, but I am absolutely compelled to do so if I want to achieve sleep or protect myself against otherwise almost unbearable pain." This essentially female "voluptuousness" is associated with what he calls "Blessedness," a state free of the divisions of hyperconsciousness and therefore infused with the sentiment of being (e.g., M, 111). Femininity stands, then, for the sensual as against the intellectual, "Blessedness" as against the insidious anxieties of "compulsive thinking," the body as against the self-torturing mind. Tactile voluptuousness is capable of dissolving, at least for a moment, the alienated, scrutinizing consciousness of Schreber's quasi-solipsism, causing him to oscillate between different physical states: "My bodily state is difficult to describe; usually there is a very rapid change between high grade bodily well-being and all sorts of more or less painful and disagreeable states" (M, 201).

Touching himself was not, however, Schreber's sole way of bringing about his own feminization; another method may have come more naturally to him. As Schreber lay in bed caressing himself, his thoughts sometimes drifted: he would find himself imagining himself elsewhere, usually standing before a mirror gazing at his own feminized body—thereby replacing actual tactile sensation by imagining a situation that he had often performed in reality (M, 181). The feminization that occurred in these moments before the mirror—whether imagined from bed or staged before the glass—was a feminization-at-a-distance, and it seems to be even more explicitly epistemological in nature: femaleness not as a lived and kinesthetic bodily presence but as a kind of epistemic objecthood. Of his mirror experiences, Schreber says, "I have *very good and important reasons* for this behaviour, however stupid or even despicable it may appear to other people" (M, 300).[15] "I consider it my right and in a certain sense my duty to cultivate feminine feelings," and "mere low sensuousness can therefore not be considered a motive in my case" (M, 207–8). One likely motive for this feminization is the desire to attain the solidity of objecthood, the ontological grounding of what Sartre calls the "in-itself." Feminization of this sort implies giving up aspirations toward being a constituting center and choosing instead the rather different form of power inherent in the role of attracting and fixing the attention of an other.[16]

So far I have been focusing on Schreber's sense of identification with his feminized reflection in the mirror, a representing of himself that he attributes to God's distant rays. A moment's thought makes it clear, however, that Schreber was actually playing the roles of both subject and object. After all, who but Schreber himself was standing before the mirror staring at himself? Who if not Schreber was the "one" carrying out this representing? I have already discussed the peculiar identity of God's consciousness ("I Who am distant"; M, 160n) with Schreber's alienated experience of his own mind. It is, then, only at the more obvious level that the mirror experience expresses Schreber's sense of being transformed into (female) object. On another, more implicit plane, this moment before the mirror also expresses his experience of himself as the "one," the male and godlike being who is capable of carrying out such a constituting transformation (and this may be doubly true when the moment is only imagined—then he is responsible both for the entire scene and for the transformation, the feminizing seeing-as, that occurs within it). Unlike the tactile voluptuousness, this feminization before the mirror does not negate the mind in the act of establishing a sense of objecthood. Both forms of feminization, tactile and visual, help to overcome the ontological queasiness of the solipsistic world, but the latter, visual type corresponds more closely to the usual structure of Schreber's being: here his passivity and objecthood can be epistemological rather than sensual, and the inner division of his self-consciousness need not be dissolved.

Schreber's curious identification and alliance with the male, godlike being who is also his oppressor emerges in the following, richly suggestive passages—allowing us to glimpse, as if through a glass darkly, the paradoxical, involutional essence of his world:

> perhaps, using an oxymoron, God Himself was on my side in His fight against me, that is to say I was able to bring His attributes and powers into battle as an effective weapon in my self-defence. (M, 79n)[17]

> of recent times in an attempt to reverse the facts I myself have been "represented" as the one who committed soul murder. (M, 55)

The self-reflexive nature of Schreber's experience was clearly a source of both danger and security, both misery and bliss. Living the roles of both subject and object sometimes felt unnatural and self-destructive, as when Schreber maintained that he had eaten part of his larynx with his food (M, 272), but it could also be a source of ecstasy:

> But as soon as I am alone with God, if I may so express myself, I must continually or at least at certain times, strive to give divine rays the impression of a woman in the height of sensual delight; to achieve this I have to employ all possible means, and have to strain all my intellectual powers and foremost my imagination. . . . *For me such moral limits to voluptuousness no longer exist, indeed in a certain sense the reverse applies.* In order not to be misunderstood, I must point out that when I speak of my duty to cultivate voluptuousness, *I never mean any sexual desires towards other human beings (females) least of all sexual intercourse,* but I have to imagine myself as man and woman in one person having intercourse with myself, or somehow have to achieve with myself a certain sexual excitement, etc . . . but which has nothing whatever to do with any idea of masturbation or anything like it. (M, 208)

Freud viewed such fantasies of bisexuality, which are not uncommon in schizophrenia, as being essentially libidinal and primitive. He spoke of "a libido located at a stage even earlier than autoeroticism" and wrote that Schreber's divine rays were "a concrete representation and external projection of libidinal cathexes."[18] Meaning, of course, is overdetermined, especially in worlds as complex as Schreber's, and there may well be some truth in this classical interpretation. But it should be apparent by now that to stop at this level of interpretation would be to miss a crucial dimension. I think we must take Schreber at his word when he insists that these fantasies—which, he says, "strain all my intellectual powers and foremost my imagination"—are not fundamentally sexual in nature, not a matter of "mere low sensuousness." A purely libidinal interpretation misses the crucial sense in which such schizophrenic fantasies concern not sex but knowledge, expressing a yearning no less intense, and no less pervasive, for being epistemological at its core.

The mirror experience, whether real or imagined, can be read as the ultimate fantasy of solipsistic self-sufficiency—one that transcends solipsism's lived contradictions. In this moment of seeing-as, all the elements of the epistemological fantasy come together, and Schreber's existence is central in every possible way. Then he feels "God's rays," the rays of his own (masculine) consciousness, as the literal creators of the world; the feminization, a matter of seeing-as, depends on them. But instead of that dissipation of selfhood that can accompany the solipsistic experience, Schreber, standing before his reflection, confronts an image of his own solidity. And, unlike tactile voluptuousness—in which self-consciousness dissolves in the stroking of his own (female) nerves—this mirrored feminization-at-a-distance is less an escape from than an apotheosis of the divided self of cerebral, hyperreflexive awareness. For this, truly, is the yearned-for final stage of the solipsistic minuet—that impossible moment when the self plays both subject and object, but without dissolving the self or collapsing the distance on which subject and object depend. Only before the mirror, as both man and woman, can Schreber become that ultimate, almost inconceivable being—an "I Who am distant."

NOTES

INTRODUCTION

1. Karl Jaspers, *General Psychopathology*, trans. J. Hoenig and Marian Hamilton (Chicago: University of Chicago Press, 1963), p. 93.

2. On the descriptive psychiatric approach, see, for example, American Psychiatric Association, *Diagnostic and Statistical Manual of Mental Disorders*, 3d ed., revised (Washington, D.C.: American Psychiatric Association, 1987), known as *DSM-III-R*. The term "psychotic" is defined as "gross impairment of reality testing and the creation of a new reality," a condition in which a person "incorrectly evaluates the accuracy of his or her perceptions and thoughts and makes incorrect inferences about external reality, even in the face of contrary evidence" (p. 404). "Hallucination" is defined as a "sensory perception without external stimulation of the relevant organ [and having] the immediate sense of reality of a true perception" (p. 398). "Delusion," defined (in brief) as "a false personal belief based on incorrect inference about external reality" (p. 395), is the key symptom for defining madness (psychosis), for, as *DSM-III-R* explains, "hallucinations indicate a psychotic disturbance only when they are associated with a gross impairment in reality testing," that is, when the "hallucination [gives] rise to the delusion that the perception is true" (p. 395). For fuller *DSM-III-R* definition of "delusion," see beginning of Chapter 1.

On the psychoanalytic approach, see the important article by John Frosch,

"The Psychotic Character," *Psychiatric Quarterly* 38 (1975), 81–96. Otto Kernberg, an influential contemporary psychoanalyst, argues that the presence or absence of the capacity for reality-testing constitutes a quite distinct boundary marker between psychotic and nonpsychotic (e.g., borderline) conditions: "Loss of reality-testing in any one area indicates psychotic functioning. . . . there is no continuum, no gradual shift from presence to absence of reality-testing; *Borderline Conditions and Pathological Narcissism* (New York: Aronson, 1975), p. 182.

3. Paul Federn, *Ego Psychology and the Psychoses* (London: Maresfield Reprints, 1977), p. 229. Two recent articles which *have* questioned the standard view of delusion are, G. E. Berrios, "Delusions as 'Wrong Beliefs': A Conceptual History," *British Journal of Psychiatry*, 159, suppl. 14 (1991), 6–13; and M. Spitzer, "On Defining Delusions," *Comprehensive Psychiatry*, 31 (1990), 377–97.

4. See Walter Kaiser, "Wisdom of the Fool," in *Dictionary of the History of Ideas*, vol. 4 (New York: Scribner's, 1973), pp. 515–20.

5. See Michel Foucault, *Madness and Civilization: A History of Insanity in the Age of Reason*, trans. Richard Howard (New York: New American Library, 1967). Foucault quotes the eighteenth-century *Encyclopédie* (1750–80): to depart from reason "with confidence and in the firm conviction that one is following it—that, it seems to me, is what is called being *mad*" (p. 91). Descartes had a similar view, for he believed that madness, like dreaming, was one of many forms of error. Foucault describes this Enlightenment perspective as follows: "Those who are delirious must be torn from this quasi-sleep, recalled from their waking dream and its images to an authentic awakening, where the dream disappears before the images of perception." On this view, such an awakening from madness occurs "in the very awareness of the dream, in the consciousness of deluded consciousness," for it is this self-reflexive condition that the madman supposedly lacks (pp. 151–52). See also Roy Porter, *Mind Forg'd Manacles: A History of Madness in England from the Restoration to the Regency* (Cambridge: Harvard University Press, 1987), pp. 187–95.

6. The connection between madness and error is implicit in the German language, in the relationship among the words *irren* (to err), *Irrtum* (error, mistake), and *Irrsinn* (insanity, madness); see Zvi Lothane, *In Defense of Schreber: Soul Murder and Psychiatry* (Hillsdale, N.J.: Analytic Press, 1992), p. 312, n. 53.

Incidentally, one might wish to criticize the cognitivist implications of the phrase "reality testing," which seems to imply some kind of explicit process of confirming a representation of or hypothesis about the external world. According to the existential-phenomenological tradition (and also, it seems, according to Wittgenstein in *On Certainty*), reality is normally taken for granted in a much more immediate fashion than this: one is simply attuned to it, and explicit testing is a more unusual event. This distinction is not generally made, however, in either the descriptive-psychiatric or the psychoanalytic tradition, where "impairment of reality testing" can refer to mistakenness involving either explicit beliefs or implicit assumptions regarding objective reality. A critique of the Cartesian and cognitivist implications of the concept of poor reality testing would be interesting but is beyond the scope of this book.

7. See Thomas Szasz, *Schizophrenia: The Sacred Symbol of Psychiatry* (New York: Basic, 1976); Michel Foucault, *The Order of Things: An Archaeology of the Human Sciences* (New York: Vintage, 1973), p. 375. Adolf Meyer wrote that "the history of dementia praecox is really that of psychiatry as a whole" (quoted at M, 14). Also see Sander Gilman, "The Mad as Artists," in *Difference and Pathology* (Ithaca: Cornell University Press, 1985), p. 225, on the fact that by the end of the nineteenth century (the beginning of the modern psychiatric era) dementia praecox had become the paradigmatic form of madness. Incidentally, the term "dementia praecox" was coined by Bénédict-Augustin Morel in 1856 and popularized by Emil Kraepelin's text published in 1896. In his influential monograph of 1911, *Dementia Praecox or the Group of Schizophrenias*, trans. Joseph Zinkin (New York: International Universities Press, 1950), Eugen Bleuler refined Kraepelin's conception of the category and renamed it "schizophrenia."

8. Bleuler, *Dementia Praecox*, p. 129.

9. Quotations are from Bleuler, *Dementia Praecox*, pp. 127–28.

10. Jaspers, *General Psychopathology*, pp. 96, 97, 105; also see pp. 93–107. Jaspers writes: "We should look at *what* it is that is actually incorrigible. . . . With these patients persecution does not always appear quite like the experience of people who are in fact being persecuted; nor does their jealousy seem like that of some justifiably jealous person, although there is often some similarity of behavior" (p. 105).

11. On overvalued ideas, see *DSM-III-R*, pp. 395, 402. See also P. J. McKenna, "Disorders with Overvalued Ideas." *British Journal of Psychiatry* 145 (1984), 579–85, esp. 579 and 583; and Jaspers, *General Psychopathology*, pp. 107, 135.

12. Jaspers, *General Psychopathology*, pp. 98–104.

13. For de Chirico's evocative descriptions of the mood state he was in while painting these works, see his writings in *The Autobiography of Surrealism*, ed. Marcel Jean (New York: Viking, 1980), pp. 2–10.

14. Jaspers, *General Psychopathology*, p. 106. "It is most important to free ourselves from this prejudice that there has to be some poverty of intelligence at the root of [delusions]," writes Jaspers (p. 97).

15. Ibid., p. 105. Actually, Jaspers considered the definitive feature of delusion proper or primary delusion (the kind found in schizophrenia) to be its incomprehensibility—the fact that, unlike a normal belief, overvalued idea, or delusion-like idea, it defies empathic understanding. The other aspects or features he mentions—such as incorrigibility and impossible content—are highly characteristic of the true delusion, but they are not its essential criterion. See ibid., pp. 95–98, and Chris Walker, "Delusion: What Did Jaspers Really Say?" *British Journal of Psychiatry* 159, suppl. 14 (1991), 94–103.

The phrase "axiom of the abyss" is from Helm Stierlin, "Karl Jaspers' Psychiatry in the Light of His Basic Philosophical Position," *Journal of the History of the Behavioral Sciences* 10 (1974), 213–26. Another influential statement of the notion that the best criterion of schizophrenia is the sense of estrangement such patients evoke can be found in H. C. Rümke, "The Nuclear Symptom of Schizophrenia and the Praecoxfeeling" (1941), trans. J. Neeleman, *History of Psychiatry* 1 (1990), 331–41. For a psychoanalytic version of this doctrine, see Ping-Nie Pao, *Schizophrenic Disorders: Theory and Treatment from a Psychodynamic Point of View* (New York: International Universities Press, 1979), pp. 13–19.

16. Notice that Schreber describes himself as having *Nervenkrankheit*, a disease of the nerves, not *Geisteskrankheit*, psychosis or mental illness; see M. 200, 286, and Lothane, *In Defense of Schreber*, p. 399. A more accurate translation of the title of Schreber's book might be *Great Thoughts of a Nervous Patient*; see Lothane, pp. 1–2.

17. Elias Canetti, *The Conscience of Words*, trans. Joachim Neugroschel (New York: Farrar, Straus and Giroux, 1979), p. 25. As the translators of the *Memoirs* note, "Schreber is now the most frequently quoted patient in psychiatry," mentioned in nearly all textbooks of psychiatry (M, 8, 11).

18. According to F. C. Redlich, "Most of the . . . psychological propositions about schizophrenia . . . may be traced back to . . . Freud's ingenious discussion of the Schreber case"; Redlich, "The Concept of Schizophrenia and Its Implications for Therapy," in *Psychotherapy with Schizophrenics*, ed. E. B. Brody and F. C. Redlich (New York, 1952)—quoted at M, 11.

19. See, for example, Bleuler, *Dementia Praecox*; Jaspers, *General Psychopathology* (where Jaspers offers Schreber as a clear illustration of schizophrenic incomprehensibility); and Jung, *Psychology of Dementia Praecox* (Princeton: Princeton University Press, 1960; orig. 1907). See also M, 8–11. Incidentally, dementia paranoides was Kraepelin's term for dementia praecox of the paranoid type; see Lothane, *In Defense of Schreber*, p. 328.

20. See, for example, the official *DSM-III-R Casebook*, in which Schreber is given the diagnosis Schizophrenia, Undifferentiated Type, Chronic (paranoid and catatonic symptoms are noted but not considered sufficiently consistent or dominant to justify subtyping Schreber as a paranoid or catatonic schizophrenic); Robert L. Spitzer, Miriam Gibbon, Andrew E. Skodol, Janet B. W. Williams, and Michael B. First, eds., *DSM-III-R Casebook* (Washington, D.C.: American Psychiatric Press, 1989), pp. 472–74. See also Irving I. Gottesman's *Schizophrenia Genesis: The Origins of Madness* (New York: Freeman, 1991), in which Schreber is offered as one of several illustrative examples of schizophrenia (pp. 59, 261).

Although most classical and contemporary experts consider Schreber to be schizophrenic (in fact, a paradigm case of the illness, albeit a case of "late-onset schizophrenia"—which is described in M. J. Harris and D. V. Jeste, "Late-Onset Schizophrenia: An Overview," *Schizophrenia Bulletin* 14 [1988], 39–56), the diagnosis has nevertheless been questioned on occasion, in recent years by psychiatrists who think Schreber should rather be considered to have suffered from major affective illness. Alan A. Lipton, for example, argues that in *DSM-III* terms Schreber better fits the diagnostic category of Major Depression with Mood Incongruent Delusions (though Lipton also acknowledges that the diagnosis Schizoaffective Disorder might be appropriate—that is, a disorder combining schizophrenic with affective features); see "Was the 'Nervous Illness' of Schreber a Case of Affective Disorder," *American Journal of Psychiatry* 141 (1984), 1236–39. Lothane makes a similar argument in *In Defense of Schreber*; see p. 432.

In a convincing reply, Kenneth S. Kendler and Robert L. Spitzer rebut Lipton's understanding both of *DSM-III* and of Schreber, clearly showing that the illness—at least as it was manifested after 1893 (i.e., during the time described in the *Memoirs*)—is a clear case of schizophrenia, with "deterioration in functioning; marked auditory hallucinations; bizarre, grandiose, paranoid, and somatic delusions; hallucinations of voices conversing; thought-insertion; made feelings and made actions; somatic passivity [these last being Schneiderian first-rank symptoms of schizophrenia]; catatonic episodes; and other bizarre behavior" and without "evidence of a full affective syndrome"; see "A Reevaluation of Schreber's Case: Letter," *American Journal of Psychiatry* 142 (1985), 1121–22. It should be noted that Spitzer was one of the main formulators of *DSM-III* and that the *DSM-III* criteria for schizophrenia are among the narrowest offered by any diagnostic system.

In another useful analysis, using Research Diagnostic Criteria, Karl G. Koehler argues that though Schreber's second, lengthy bout of illness (nine years of hospitalization, from 1893 to 1902) began as mostly affective in nature, it quickly developed schizophrenic features, then resolved into a chronic paranoid schizophrenic syndrome; see "The Schreber Case and Affective Illness: A Research Diagnostic Re-Assessment," *Psychological Medicine 11* (1981), 689–96. Schreber's *Memoirs*, and hence my analysis in this book, is entirely devoted to the second phase.

For the purposes of my argument, these diagnostic controversies are somewhat beside the point. The disagreements derive, to a large extent, from different ways of conceptualizing the diagnosis, with Lipton, for example, tending to prefer a longitudinal perspective that concentrates on course of illness to the relative exclusion of presenting symptoms (see Lipton, p. 1238). Though I do not believe there is any one correct definition of schizophrenia, in this book I use the term in a way that places primary emphasis on the symptomatic picture. From this standpoint, at least, it can hardly be disputed that Schreber manifested psychological symptoms that have widely and traditionally been associated with schizophrenia. Those who think Schreber merits a different diagnosis need not dismiss my phenomenological interpretation on these grounds, however; they might simply think of the interpretation as applying not to schizophrenia per se so much as to instances of what might be called schizophrenia-like or schizophreniform symptoms.

21. In his lectures in the early 1930s, Wittgenstein emphasized the importance of recognizing that, though one might wish to call his thinking a form of philosophy, he was not doing the same kind of thing as, say, Plato or Berkeley had done. Wittgenstein said that his work constituted a "new subject" (sometimes he called it "modern philosophy"), meant to take the place of philosophy as traditionally conceived—not merely another stage in "a continuous development" of philosophy but a "kink" in the "development of human thought" (L, 9, 26).

22. See Kaiser, "Wisdom of the Fool," p. 519.

23. See P. M. S. Hacker, *Insight and Illusion: Wittgenstein on Philosophy and the Metaphysics of Experience* (London: Oxford University Press, 1972), pp. 185–86, 216.

24. The phrase "form of life" is taken from Wittgenstein; see, e.g., *Philosophical Investigations*, §19; 226.

25. For this reason the controversial question of what role Schreber's upbringing, and particularly his father, may have played in the *development* of his symptoms is not taken up in the text; but see Chapter 2, n. 45 and Conclusion, n. 5. Concerning neurobiological underpinnings, see the appendix of Louis A. Sass, *Madness and Modernism: Insanity in the Light of Modern Art, Literature, and Thought* (New York: Basic Books, 1992).

26. Quoted in Eugene Meyer and Lino Covi, "The Experience of Depersonalization: A Written Report by a Patient," *Psychiatry* 23 (1960), 215.

27. But see the suggestive footnote in Stanley Cavell, "The Availability of Wittgenstein's Later Philosophy," in *Must We Mean What We Say?* (Cambridge: Cambridge University Press, 1976), p. 67n. See also Karen Hanson's remarks in "Being Doubted, Being Assured," in *Images in our Souls: Cavell, Psychoanalysis, and Cinema*, ed. Joseph H. Smith and William Kerrigan (Baltimore: Johns Hopkins University Press, 1987), pp. 187–202.

28. A particularly clear expression of this view can be found in Julian Jaynes, *The Origins of Consciousness in the Breakdown of the Bicameral Mind* (Boston: Houghton Mifflin, 1976), pp. 414–16, 432. Jaynes interprets Schreber's schizophrenia as the emergence of the "primitive mental organization" of the "archaic, bicameral mind," which is supposedly devoid of awareness of itself as mind. Psychoanalytic versions of the primitivity interpretation of schizophrenia can be found in Thomas Freeman, John Cameron, and Andrew McGhie, *Chronic Schizophrenia* (New York: International Universities Press, 1958); Sidney J. Blatt and Cynthia Wild, *Schizophrenia: A Developmental Analysis* (New York: Academic Press, 1976); Otto Fenichel, *The Psychoanalytic Theory of Neurosis* (New York: Norton, 1945), pp. 415–52; Silvano Arieti, *The Interpretation of Schizophrenia* 2d ed. (New York: Basic, 1974). See also Heinz Werner, *Comparative Psychology of Mental Development* (New York: International Universities Press, 1957).

29. See, for example, Norman O. Brown, *Love's Body* (New York: Vintage, 1966), pp. 248–54; Gilles Deleuze and Félix Guattari, *Anti-Oedipus: Capitalism and Schizophrenia* (New York: Viking, 1977); R. D. Laing, *The Politics of Experience* (New York: Penguin, 1967). Incidentally, Laing's first and in my view best book on schizophrenia, *The Divided Self* (Harmondsworth: Penguin, 1965), does not engage in the kind of romantic glorification found in certain of his later works.

30. Freud argued that psychosis involves an overcoming of the ego by the id, thus, dominance of the personality by affective and instinctual processes; see, for example, "Neurosis and Psychosis" (1924), in *General Psychological Theory*, ed. Philip Rieff (New York: Collier/Macmillan, 1963), 185–89. In many of his writings, however, Freud also emphasized a process of *detachment* of libido—a position that certainly sounds, on the face of it, similar to the one I am espousing by referring to detachment from emotion and desire. In the view of Freud and many other analysts, however, libidinal motivations are not attenuated but only redirected; thus, although libido is detached from *external* objects (a process supposedly facilitated by the dominance of the unrealistic id), it is then turned on the self (this is how Freud accounts, for example, for the megalomaniacal symptoms of many psychotics); see, for example, Freud's study (pub. 1911) of Schreber, "Psychoanaly-

tic Notes upon an Autobiographical Account of a Case of Paranoia (Dementia Paranoides)," in *Three Case Histories*, ed. Philip Rieff (New York: Collier/Macmillan, 1963), pp. 174–76, 179–80; and "On Narcissism: An Introduction" (1914), in *General Psychological Theory*, p. 67. See also Ping-Nie Pao, *Schizophrenic Disorders*, pp. 41–53.

Victor Tausk accounts for the hypochondriacal preoccupations of schizophrenics in similar fashion, by interpreting them as resulting from the "influx of libido" into the bodily self that supposedly occurs when libidinal interest is withdrawn from the outer world. Tausk is then forced to offer a rather elaborate theoretical account of why these hypochondriacal symptoms in schizophrenia are so often accompanied by feelings of *estrangement* from, rather than pleasure in, the bodily self: he argues that the estrangement is a consequence of "a defense against [this] libidinal cathexis" (i.e., a defense against a defense); see Tausk, "On the Origin of the 'Influencing Machine' in Schizophrenia," *The Psychoanalytic Quarterly* 2 (1933), 519–56, quotation from 549–50. See the conclusion of this book for further discussion of the difference between the psychoanalytic view and my epistemological one, which does not view the schizophrenic's lived-world or sense of self as dominated by libido or desire. See also Chap. 1, nn. 21, 62.

31. John Wisdom quoted in Alice Ambrose, "Ludwig Wittgenstein: A Portrait," in *Ludwig Wittgenstein: Philosophy and Language*, ed. Alice Ambrose and Morris Lazerowitz (London: Allen and Unwin, 1972), pp. 17–18.

32. Hermine Wittgenstein, "My Brother Ludwig," in *Recollections of Wittgenstein*, 2d ed., ed. Rush Rhees (New York: Oxford University Press, 1984), p. 4. Hermine also mentions how, at a period when her brother was working on one of his first pieces of philosophical writing, he was "in a constant, indescribable, almost pathological state of agitation" (p. 2).

33. Cavell, "The Availability of Wittgenstein's Later Philosophy," p. 71.

34. Various criteria—including the form of the symptomatology (my focus in this study), course of the illness, and drug responsitivity—can be used to define the schizophrenic diagnosis, and various external validators—such as family history of psychiatric illness, biological tests, and the presence of related symptoms—can be used to test these diagnoses. Choice of both criteria and validators is based largely on value judgments, assessments of which characterization of the disorder is most conceptually appealing. There is no reason to assume that the validators are or could be interchangeable or that, with sufficient empirical research, the sets of diagnostic criteria will eventually converge, all selecting the same subpopulation as meriting the diagnosis. For an excellent discussion of the unavoidably theoretical nature of arguments about the schizophrenic diagnosis, see Kenneth Kendler, "Toward a Scientific Psychiatric Nosology: Strengths and

Limitations," *Archives of General Psychiatry* 47 (1990), 969–73. On the heterogeneity of schizophrenia, see, for example, Leopold Bellak and John Strauss, eds., *Schizophrenia Bulletin* 5, no.3 (1979).

35. Kraepelin emphasized course of illness and prognosis (i.e., a chronic, deteriorating pattern) as criteria for diagnosing schizophrenia, and he viewed schizophrenia as a kind of dementia.

36. I am not necessarily accepting the notion that there is a single essence to the schizophrenia concept or that any pathognomonic features or sharp boundaries distinguish it from related disorders. It is possible that schizophrenia (as well as the solipsistic grouping studied in this book) is better understood as a kind of Wittgensteinian family concept.

37. To rely so heavily on texts written by patients, as I have done in this book, has certain obvious advantages: it spares us the potentially biasing intermediary of third-party descriptions. But it also has certain disadvantages: it is difficult, perhaps impossible, to know to what extent a written or spoken description reflects the nature of an experience as it was originally lived. Some of what one reads may be an artifact of the text, involving embellishments or transformations introduced by the patient in the act of reflection or moment of writing. But unless one wants to lapse into some kind of absolute skepticism (or into the view that there is nothing outside the text), it seems reasonable to operate on the assumption that language can and does reflect experience with reasonable accuracy. In any case, a close phenomenological analysis of a lived-world would hardly be possible in the absence of a highly elaborated autobiographical report; so, unless one is willing to give up all hope for such a project, the problem of the artifact is largely unavoidable. (See Jaspers, *General Psychopathology*, p. 55.)

I have done what I could to support the plausibility of my reading by bringing in examples from other, similar patients (in the text as well as in the notes), sometimes autobiographical accounts, other times descriptions by external observers. The general adequacy and coherence of this reading of schizophrenic symptoms should help to support my interpretation of Schreber's text.

38. I doubt that this "solipsistic" group closely matches any of the well-known current subgroupings of schizophrenia, such as paranoid as opposed to nonparanoid, or patients with "positive" as opposed to "negative" symptoms. It is possible, however, that my interpretation is most adequate for those patients who would be called "introjective" rather than "anaclitic" according to one interesting, but not widely accepted, subclassification scheme; see Sidney Blatt and S. Schichman, "Two Primary Configurations of Pathology," *Psychoanalysis and Contemporary Thought* 6 (1983), 187–254.

39. This situation—in which descriptions also function as, or aspire toward being, definitions—is actually common in theoretical writings on pathological types, a fact that, according to Wittgenstein, is inevitable and not to be deplored. See Wittgenstein's discussions in his later writings of the ambiguity of what he calls "criteria" (a much discussed term that Wittgenstein uses to refer to defining or in some sense essential characteristics) and "symptoms" (i.e., commonly associated features)—for example, in *The Blue and Brown Books*, where he writes: "Doctors will use names of diseases without ever deciding which phenomena are to be taken as criteria and which as symptoms; and this need not be a deplorable lack of clarity. For remember that in general we don't use language according to strict rules—it hasn't been taught to us by means of strict rules, either" (BBB, 25).

1. A MIND'S EYE WORLD

1. See American Psychiatric Association, *Diagnostic and Statistical Manual of Mental Disorders,* 3d ed. *(DSM-III),* (Washington, D.C., American Psychiatric Association, 1980), p. 356; see also 3d ed., revised (*DSM-III-R)* 1987, pp. 395.

On the conception of delusions as fixed false beliefs in *DSM-IV*, planned for 1994, see Michael Flaum and Nancy C. Andreasen, "Diagnostic Criteria for Schizophrenia and Related Disorders: Options for DSM-IV," *Schizophrenia Bulletin* 17 (1991), 133–56, esp. 146, 150.

2. Eugen Bleuler, "Autistic Thinking" (1912), reprinted in *Organization and Pathology of Thought*, ed. and trans. David Rapaport (New York: Columbia University Press, 1951), pp. 401–2.

3. Georg Büchner, *Leonce and Lena; Lenz; Woyzeck*, trans. Michael Hamburger (Chicago: University of Chicago Press, 1972), p. 5.

4. Sandor Ferenczi and Otto Rank, quoted in James Glass, "I am the Curator of Delusion," *Psychoanalysis and Contemporary Thought* 4 (1981), 569. Second quotation from Thomas Freeman, *Psychopathology of the Psychoses* (New York: International Universities Press, 1969), p. 163. Ferenczi (1916) believed that the schizophrenic experiences "the hallucinatory omnipotence of the small child"; quoted in Glass, "I am the Curator," p. 569. According to a review article on psychotherapy with schizophrenics, no one considers schizophrenic and infantile mental structure and functioning to be identical, but most writers "maintain that in regression, states of mind more primitive chronologically and developmentally gain ascendancy and that these states resemble, in structure and function, those postulated to be operative during infancy and early childhood"; Thomas McGlashan, "Intensive Individual Psychotherapy of Schizophrenia," *Archives of General Psychiatry* 40 (1983), 911.

5. See A. N. Applebee, *The Child's Concept of Story* (Chicago: University of Chicago Press, 1978), and John H. Flavell, "The Development of Children's Knowledge about the Appearance-Reality Distinction," *American Psychologist* 41 (1986), 418–25.

6. Harold Searles, "The Differentiation between Concrete and Metaphorical Thinking in the Recovering Schizophrenic Patient," in *Collected Papers on Schizophrenia and Related Subjects* (New York: International Universities Press, 1965), pp. 560–83, quotations from pp. 574–75, 568.

7. The analyst Robert White, for example, interpreted Schreber as dominated by "pregenital destructive impulses" and "primitive pregenital procreation fantasies"; "The Mother-Conflict in Schreber's Psychosis," *International Journal of Psychoanalysis* 42 (1961), 55–73, esp. 55–56. Freud himself considered schizophrenics to be fixated at a stage even earlier than autoeroticism; see Victor Tausk, "On the Origin of the Influencing Machine in Schizophrenia" (1919), *Psychoanalytic Quarterly* 2 (1933), 519–56, esp. 542. Ernst Kris describes the psychotic condition as a state "in which the ego is overwhelmed by the primary process"; *Psychoanalytic Explorations in Art* (New York: Schocken, 1964), p. 60.

8. Marguerite Sechehaye, *A New Psychotherapy in Schizophrenia* (New York: Grune and Stratton, 1956), p. 149.

9. The words are those of Sylvère Lotringer, from "Libido Unbound: The Politics of 'Schizophrenia'," in "Anti-Oedipus," *Semiotexte* 2, no. 3 (1977), 8–10.

10. Bronislaw Malinowski, *Argonauts of the Western Pacific* (London: George Routledge and Sons, 1932), p. 10. Claude Lévi-Strauss, *Savage Mind* (Chicago: University of Chicago Press, 1966), p. 42. My thesis in this book bears a certain resemblance to that of Lévi-Strauss's *The Savage Mind*, where it is argued that the very features of tribal thought previously assumed to be primitive and Dionysian are in fact highly complex, sophisticated, and cognitive in their motivation.

11. Even during his psychotic period (which had a schizophrenic-like quality, even though his psychosis was not a straightforward case of schizophrenia), Friedrich Nietzsche had a pervasively ironic quality. Shortly after his psychotic break, he wrote the following in a letter to his friend, the historian Jacob Burckhardt: "Dear Herr Professor, when it comes to it I too would very much prefer a professorial chair in Basle to being God; but I did not dare to go as far in my private egoism as to refrain for its sake from the creation of the world." Nietzsche also refers to himself as "being condemned to entertain the next eternity with bad witticisms"; quoted in Erich Heller, "Burckhardt and Nietzsche," in *The Disinherited Mind* (New York: Harcourt Brace Jovanovich, 1975), p. 83. Also see Gerhard Kloos, "Über den

Witz der Schizophrenen," *Zeitschrift für die gesamte Neurologie und Psychiatrie* 172 (1941), 536–77; W. Mayer-Gross, "Über Spiel, Scherz, Ironie und Humor in der Schizophrenie," *Zeitschrift für die gesamte Neurologie und Psychiatrie* 69 (1921), 332–53; and Louis A. Sass, *Madness and Modernism* (New York: Basic Books, 1992), pp. 112–15.

12. Manfred Bleuler, *The Schizophrenic Disorders* (New Haven: Yale University Press, 1978), p. 488.

13. Eugen Bleuler, *Dementia Praecox or the Group of Schizophrenias*, trans. Joseph Zinkin (New York: International Universities Press, 1950), p. 113. The author of *The Autobiography of a Schizophrenic Girl*, ed. Marguerite Sechehaye (New York: New American Library, 1970), whose pseudonym is Renée, reports that "the noises, localized on the right side, drove me to stop up my ears. But I readily distinguished them from the noises of reality. I heard them without hearing them and recognized that they arose within me" (p. 42).

14. See Bleuler, *Dementia Praecox*, pp. 65, 127–30.

15. Kurt Schneider, *Clinical Psychopathology* (New York: Grune and Stratton, 1959), pp. 88–145. See also C. S. Mellor, "First Rank Symptoms of Schizophrenia," *British Journal of Psychiatry* 117 (1970), 15–23. *DSM-III* and *DSM-III-R* incorporate elements of Schneider's system in their criteria for the schizophrenic diagnosis. For a cogent defense of Schneider's approach against its detractors, see J. Hoenig, "Schneider's First Rank Symptoms and the Tabulators," *Comprehensive Psychiatry* 25 (1984), 77–87.

16. Barbara O'Brien, *Operators and Things* (Cambridge, Mass.: Arlington, 1958), p. 11.

17. Karl Jaspers, *General Psychopathology*, trans. J. Hoenig and Marian W. Hamilton (Chicago: University of Chicago Press, 1963), pp. 107–8.

18. Of the last three examples, two are mentioned in Bleuler, *Dementia Praecox*, pp. 141, 124; one in Heinz Werner, *Comparative Psychology of Mental Development* (New York: International Universities Press, 1957), p. 370.

19. Bleuler, *Dementia Praecox*, p. 41.

20. Patient quoted in Eugene Meyer and Lino Covi, "The Experience of Depersonalization: A Written Report by a Patient," *Psychiatry* 23 (1960), 215–16.

21. Sechehaye, *Autobiography of a Schizophrenic Girl*, p. 60. Paul Federn, "Narcissism in the Structure of the Ego," in *Ego Psychology and the Psychoses* (London: Maresfield Reprints, 1977), p. 40. Most psychoanalysts have interpreted this devitalization as a secondary phenomenon, a defense against the overwhelming encroachments of the id; see, for example, Otto Fenichel, *The Psychoanalytic Theory of Neurosis* (New York: Norton,

1945), pp. 417–20; McGlashan, "Intensive Individual Psychotherapy," p. 914; Tausk, "Origin of the Influencing Machine," pp. 549–50. Yet it seems to be such a fundamental aspect of the illness, and so characteristic of the early phases of the illness, that one might question the appropriateness of this interpretation. See n. 62 for related discussion.

22. The first statement ("my so-called children") was made by a schizophrenic patient treated by a colleague. The second is from Thomas Freeman, John L. Cameron, and Andrew McGhie, *Chronic Schizophrenia* (New York: International Universities Press, 1958), p. 62.

Some schizoid and schizophrenic patients experience this feeling of unreality as attaching to everything around them. Mr. Y, a patient of the psychoanalyst Charles Rycroft, experienced the realms of both the imaginary and the real as having a quasi-solipsistic quality of hypotheticalness. Was that really Dr. Rycroft who sat there talking to him? Possibly yes, possibly no, but it did not really matter since it was a purely hypothetical issue in any case. Was the patient actually the son of Khrushchev, Eisenhower, and Joe Louis, as he fantasized? This too was only a hypothetical matter to him. According to Rycroft, the patient at times "formulated clearly and intelligently the idea that his thoughts were the only reality, and that when he thought, his thoughts were the world in action . . . an idea which only someone who is God can reasonably hold." Also, Mr. Y sometimes equated the universe with his own body, as if "the only real events were those which occurred in his alimentary canal, his vascular system, or his brain"; Rycroft, "On the Defensive Function of Schizophrenic Thinking and Delusion-Formation," in *Imagination and Reality* (New York: International Universities Press, 1958), pp. 84–101, quotation from p. 94.

23. Jonathan Lang, "The Other Side of Ideological Aspects of Schizophrenia," *Psychiatry* 3 (1940), 389–93. Note, incidentally, the emphasis on needing to gain "affective tone"—as if the psychosis were devoid of, rather than flooded by, the emotion and desire supposedly characteristic of the primary process.

24. R. D. Laing, *The Divided Self* (Harmondsworth: Penguin, 1965), p. 158.

25. Here are certain crucial phrases in the original German: "Zu den Zeiten der Annäherung gewährt meine Brust den Eindruck eines ziemlich voll entwickelten weiblichen Busens . . . jeder, der mich mit entblösstem oberen Teile des Rumpfes vor dem Spiegel stehen sehen würde,—zumal, wenn die Illusion durch etwas weiblichen Aufputz unterstützt wird—den unzweifelhaften Eindruck eines *weiblichen Oberkörpers*" (M, orig, 279–80).

26. "mit Hilfe meiner Einbildungskraft als ein weibliches Wesen vor-

zustellen und dieser Illusion hätte natürlich der Schnurrbart ein kaum überwindliches Hindernis bereitet" (M, orig, 196–97).

27. In *Autobiography of a Schizophrenic Girl*, the patient Renée describes a quasi-solipsistic sense that the world depends on the observer; she also mentions the feeling of isolation that tends to accompany this orientation: "At that time, according to my concept of the world, things didn't exist in and of themselves, but each one created a world after his own fashion. . . . The question of social relationships did not touch me in the slightest degree" (p. 54).

28. "sich im Wege des 'Darstellens' den Eindruck eines gewissermassen vor Blödsinn brüllenden Menschen zu verschaffen" (M, orig, 206).

29. For a useful discussion of some of these issues, see Malcolm Budd, "Wittgenstein on Seeing Aspects," *Mind* 96 (1987), 1–17.

30. The irrelevance of acts of will to standard acts of perception is expressed in the following passage: "One doesn't '*take*' what one knows as the cutlery at a meal *for* cutlery; any more than one ordinarily tries to move one's mouth as one eats, or aims at moving it" (PI, 195).

31. "Der Begriff des 'Darstellens', d. h. einer Sache oder einer Person einen anderen Anschein geben, als den sie ihrer wirklichen Natur nach hat (menschlich ausgedrückt 'des Fälschens')" (M, orig, 128n).

32. Bleuler, *Dementia Praecox*, p. 124; see also the examples on p. 126, which include a catatonic patient who experienced his bed as being both a polar bear and a bed.

33. In this sense, the aspect seeing does not teach, or attempt to teach, us anything about the external world; see RPPII, 63, 702.

34. Also see the footnote on p. 89 of the *Memoirs*, in which Schreber states that his own experience refutes the notion, asserted by Kraepelin, that "faulty judgment . . . invariably accompanies delusions." Schreber may, of course, have been motivated to exaggerate the inconsequentiality of his delusions because of his desire to avoid legal commitment. His claims are supported, however, both by the judge's assessment and by the whole tone of the *Memoirs*.

35. See TLP, § 5.62: "What solipsism *means* is quite correct . . . it shows itself. That the world is *my* world." Also see NB, 85: "As my idea is the world. . . ."

36. Perhaps the closest thing to an explicit and pure version of solipsism in the history of modern philosophy occurs in the system of the neo-Kantian idealist philosopher, Johann Gottlieb Fichte (1762–1814), who believed that the ego, "this peculiar inward power," posits both itself and the world. "In all consciousness," he wrote, "I contemplate myself, for I am myself:— to the subjective conscious being, consciousness is self-contemplation. And

the objective . . . is also myself,—the same self which contemplates, but now floating as an objective presentation before the subjective." "Strictly speaking, [there is] no *consciousness of things*, but only a *consciousness . . . of a consciousness of things*," for all knowledge is "but pictures, representations; and there is always something awanting in it,—that which corresponds to the representation." Fichte believed that the logical conclusion to be drawn was that only I myself alone exist and that the entire universe, including other human beings, is the creation of my own mind. With this vanishing of "a material world existing independently," one is "absolved . . . from all dependence." You need "no longer tremble at a necessity which exists only in thine own thought [or] fear to be crushed by things which are the product of thine own mind." Fichte went on to argue, in the final chapter of his *Vocation of Man*, that if other persons are merely dream personages then any sense of duty toward them is nonsensical and the everyday social and practical life really a kind of delirium. To act morally, taking others as conscious persons, is therefore to exhibit a kind of madness. But precisely for this reason, Fichte argues, we must *assume* the reality of other persons, since without such an assumption we could hardly live. Thus, solipsism is logically necessary but morally impossible. Indeed, for Fichte belief in the reality of other minds is, in a sense, the delusion by which one rationalizes the madness of *not* acting like a solipsist! Quotations from J. G. Fichte, *The Vocation of Man*, trans. W. Smith (Chicago: Open Court, 1910, orig. 1800), pp. 28, 70, 55, 91, 83, 106–8. Also see B. A. G. Fuller, *A History of Philosophy*, rev. ed. (New York: Holt, 1945), pp. 288–89; and Sass, *Madness and Modernism: Insanity in the Light of Modern Art, Literature, and Thought*, pp. 313–21.

37. Wittgenstein was not arguing in a reductionistic vein by claiming that all philosophers who hold such doctrines do so only because of such experiences. To say that a certain kind of experience or existential stance may, at least in certain cases, motivate (and seem to justify) the doctrines in question is not to deny that the doctrines also derive from the internal logic or intellectual history of philosophical ideas as such. Exploration of the experiential context of the doctrines is not, in itself, an attempt to offer a logical refutation of the doctrines, though it may well decrease their plausibility.

It might be argued that, as a *philosophical* doctrine, solipsism, at least in many instances, really means to leave everything just as it is; that it is intended only to offer a way of analyzing experience, not to suggest or encourage radical changes in experience itself (the same could be said for many expressions of phenomenalism and idealism). In my view, this cannot be maintained for the solipsistic (or quasi-solipsistic) doctrines of either Fichte or Schopenhauer, both of whom wished to effect some kind of existential change in one's attitude toward and relationship with external reality. The same could be said of the solipsism that tempted Wittgenstein himself during World War I (see NB, 73–84).

38. For further discussion of the incompatibility of subjectivization with an action orientation, see Part 4 of Jean-Paul Sartre's *The Psychology of Imagination*, trans. Bernard Frechtman (New York: Washington Square Press, 1966); see also Erwin Straus, "The Phenomenology of Hallucinations," in *Phenomenological Psychology: The Selected Papers of Erwin Straus*, trans. Erling Eng (New York: Basic, 1966), 277–89. Also relevant is Martin Heidegger's contrasting of the "contemplative attitude" (the *sine qua non* of Cartesian skepticism concerning the reality of the external world) with the "ordinary practical contexts of agency" in which the existence of the world is taken for granted; see Charles Guignon, *Heidegger and the Problem of Knowledge* (Indianapolis: Hackett, 1983), esp. pp. 242–43.

39. One famous connoisseur of inactivity, Marcel Proust, describes this kind of subjectivization: "When I saw any external object, my consciousness that I was seeing it would remain between me and it, enclosing it in a slender incorporeal outline which prevented me from ever coming directly in contact with the material form; for it would volatilize itself in some way before I could touch it"; quoted in Wylie Sypher, *Loss of the Self in Modern Literature and Art* (New York: Vintage, 1962), p. 60.

40. Translation corrected. Another sentence frequently uttered by the voices was "Why do you not say it (aloud)?" (M, 70n, 199), a statement that expresses Schreber's sense of the innerness and privacy of his own experience, a feeling related to his quasi-solipsism.

41. Lang, "Other Side of the Ideological Aspects," p. 392. Also see Eugene Minkowski, "Findings in a Case of Schizophrenic Depression," in *Existence*, ed. Rollo May (New York: Simon and Schuster, 1958), p. 136: "One fact must be kept in mind—as soon as [the patient] performed some action his entire attitude changed, but once the act was finished he immediately fell back into his delusions." Also see M. Alpert and K. N. Silvers, "Perceptual Characteristics Distinguishing Auditory Hallucinations in Schizophrenia and Acute Alcoholic Psychoses," *American Journal of Psychiatry*, 127 (1970), 300.

42. See discussion in P. M. S. Hacker, *Insight and Illusion: Wittgenstein on Philosophy and the Metaphysics of Experience* (London: Oxford University Press, 1972), pp. 132–33, 190.

43. In an interesting passage in the *Investigations*, Wittgenstein describes the perception of others as lacking consciousness, as being automata rather than other minds, as an act of seeing-as (PI § 420).

44. One might contrast these solipsistic experiences with Maurice Mer-

leau-Ponty's phenomenological description of the normal form of life—in which the lived world, as a locus both of meaningfulness and of substance, is felt as *our* world rather than as *my* world: "Paul and I 'together' see this landscape, we are jointly present in it, it is the same for both of us, not only as an intelligible significance, but as a certain accent of the world's style, down to its very thisness"; *Phenomenology of Perception*, trans. Colin Smith (London: Routledge and Kegan Paul, 1962), p. 406.

45. William James, *The Principles of Psychology*, Vol. 2 (Cambridge, Mass.: Harvard University Press, 1981, orig. 1890), pp. 678–79.

46. "Dagegen ist es ein wirklicher, d. h. nach der Bestimmtheit meiner Erinnerung in diesem Punkte für mich *subjektiv gewisser* Vorgang—mögen mir nun andere Menschen darin Glauben schenken können oder nicht—" (M, orig, 82).

47. Bleuler, *Dementia Praecox*, p. 41. A definition recently proposed by Manfred Spitzer, in his interesting article "On Defining Delusions" (*Comprehensive Psychiatry*, 31, [1990], 377–97), is consistent with my solipsistic interpretation. Spitzer suggests the following definition of delusions: "statements about external reality which are uttered like statements about a mental state, i.e., with subjective certainty and incorrigible by others" (p. 391). Spitzer's argument is based on purely linguistic and logical considerations, however, and he does not speculate about the mode of experience that underlies delusions. Also, he continues to assume that delusions involve an "unjustified claim for intersubjective validity" (p. 392)—which, I think, fails to capture the quasi-solipsistic quality of many schizophrenic delusions.

48. Heinz Werner, *Comparative Psychology of Mental Development*, p. 418.

49. Eugen Bleuler mentions one such patient, who seemed to dismiss the importance of locating any external source for the voices she subjectively heard. "After all, the voices may be here," the patient said (*Dementia Praecox*, p. 115). See also Straus, "Phenomenology of Hallucinations."

Not all cases of seeing with the mind's eye are instances of seeing-as in Wittgenstein's sense, by the way. As the passage just quoted (M, 117) suggests, some of the vivid impressions Schreber experiences seem to consist only of inner mental images and thus do not involve the seeing of aspects of external perceptual objects.

50. Quoted in Manfred Bleuler, *The Schizophrenic Disorders*, p. 493.

51. See, for example, the description of the schizoid personality disorder in Theodore Millon, *Disorders of Personality, DSM-III: Axis II* (New York: Wiley, 1981), pp. 273–96. Millon speaks of the schizoid person as having "defects," "deficits," or "incapacities" in the emotional sphere. According

to him, such people "lack the emotional equipment for experiencing the finer shades and subtleties of emotional life," have "an intrinsic emotional blandness and interpersonal imperceptiveness," and "rarely are introspective" (pp. 273, 274, 284).

52. This defensive interpretation is frequently made by psychoanalytic writers. See, for example, Sigmund Freud, "Psychoanalytic Notes upon an Autobiographical Account of a Case of Paranoia (Dementia Paranoides)" (1911), in *Three Case Histories*, ed. Philip Rieff (New York: Collier/Macmillan, 1963), pp. 174–80, and "On Narcissism: An Introduction" (1914), in *General Psychological Theory*, ed. Philip Rieff (New York: Collier/Macmillan, 1963), p. 67. See also the writings of the British object-relations school on the schizoid problem, for example, Harold Guntrip, *Schizoid Phenomena, Object Relations, and the Self* (New York: International Universities Press, 1968).

53. Lang, "Other Side of the Ideological Aspects," p. 392.

54. Eugene Meyer and Lino Covi, "The Experience of Depersonalization: A Written Report by a Patient," *Psychiatry* 23 (1960), 215–17.

55. I am not claiming that schizophrenics never have delusions that fit the poor reality-testing formula or that all their delusions have a quasi-solipsist quality. The point is that, in many instances, the standard interpretation fails to appreciate how their delusional claims assume not the normal horizons of experience but rather a wholly different form of life. This is especially likely to be the case with the sorts of delusions that are most distinctive of schizophrenia, those involving alteration in the very structure of consciousness or the organization of the universe—as in (most) first-rank symptoms, in paranoid/grandiose delusions about one's own centrality, about world catastrophe, and so on. It would be unwise, however, to assume too much consistency in schizophrenic experience.

56. Bleuler, *Dementia Praecox*, p. 56. Bleuler offers this as an example of how the patient "takes symbolically what the physician understands in its literal sense." For a similar example, see Sechehaye, *Autobiography of a Schizophrenic Girl*, where Renée explains that, in saying she was cold, she was referring not to being physically cold but "to my inner cold, to my desolation and to the impossibility of pulling myself together. But never, absolutely never, did I think of physical cold. My friends, however, interpreted what I said in a matter-of-fact way and to my complete amazement . . . sent me woolens" (p. 52).

As an example of how a therapist's presuppositions about primitivity and literalness can bias interpretation of a patient's remarks, consider the following excerpt in which Harold F. Searles (widely considered to be one of the most sensitive observers of schizophrenia) is undeterred by the patient's own quite explicit denial that his meaning is intended to be literal:

> One incident which helped me to understand why [the patient] was as yet unable to think in figurative terms occurred during one of the many sessions when evidently he was finding me to be discouragingly unresponsive and unmoved by his helpless plight. He commented, "Always angry—my therapist is always angry at me," and then said, in the same tone of discouragement and exasperation, that his sister had written that she had purchased some chairs for her apartment, chairs made of iron, so heavy that one could move them only with great difficulty. I replied, "And you feel, perhaps, that your therapist is like the heavy chairs—very hard to move?" He laughed as though my comment were ridiculous, saying, "No, I know you're not a chair, Dr. Searles. . . . There's a chair," he said, pointing to the chair over at my desk, "and there's Dr. Searles," he finished, pointing at me. I realized now that as yet he could just *barely* distinguish between the chair and his therapist, even at a *concrete* level. . . . His literal mode of thought . . . was a product of the tenuousness of his ego boundaries. This revealed, therefore, the defensive usefulness of his regression to a state of incomplete differentiation of ego boundaries. (Searles, "The Differentiation between Concrete and Metaphorical", p. 565)

Given that the patient explicitly denies that he confuses therapist and chair, one must ask just whose literalness is manifested here—Searles's or that of his patient. Could it be that what feels to the patient like the heavy immobility of the therapist is manifested here, in the therapist's dogged literalism in responding to the patient's words?

57. Samuel Beckett, *Murphy* (New York: Grove Press, 1957), pp. 107, 181.

58. Sechehaye, *Autobiography of a Schizophrenic Girl*, pp. 78–79.

59. See, for example, the symptoms described in Emil Kraepelin, *Dementia Praecox and Paraphrenia* (Huntington, N.Y.: Robert Krieger, 1971; facs. 1919 ed.), pp. 26–27.

60. Eugen Bleuler describes similar phenomena: a patient who has been dead three times before and now is contemplating suicide; another who is "dead and yet living"; another who "was frozen in a bathtub, yet is still here"; *Dementia Praecox*, p. 123.

61. Bleuler, *Dementia Praecox*, p. 126.

62. Incidentally, one standard psychoanalytic interpretation of affective flattening sees it as a second-order consequence of the primitivity of the schizophrenic emotional life. On this view, the affective organization of the schizophrenic involves "preverbal physiologic tension states with little psy-

chological elaboration in fantasy or cognition such that the patient is unable to know who is feeling or what is being felt. Emotions are experienced as immediate concrete reality without subtle differentiation, leading to global defenses against all affect, which renders the patient a dead-to-feeling automaton; McGlashan, "Intensive Individual Psychotherapy," p. 914.

This view has often been taken to imply that schizophrenics need to learn to distance themselves from their own experiences—for example, to develop stronger "observing egos"; see, for example, Charles Donnelly, "The Observing Self and the Development of Cohesiveness," *British Journal of Medical Psychology* 52 (1979), 277–79. My own interpretation, by contrast, views the pathology as rooted in tendencies toward detachment and self-distancing from body and world. To refute the above-mentioned psychoanalytic interpretation is, of course, difficult, if not impossible, given that the postulated stratum of primitive experience is by definition largely hidden and unobservable. The evidence for this psychoanalytic interpretation is much less compelling, however, if one gives up the assumption that psychotic pathology must be, in its essence, a manifestation of primitive modes of experience.

In some sense, however, my own approach and this kind of psychoanalytic explanation are not really in direct conflict, for they are different kinds of analysis. The thrust of my interpretation is phenomenological—concerned with describing the lived-world of schizophreniform delusion rather than with accounting for it in some metapsychological or explanatory fashion. I would, however, certainly disagree with a psychoanalyst who dismissed the solipsistic aspects as being of little importance because they are *merely* defensive. It is in fact just these solipsistic aspects that dominate the experience of many schizophrenic patients and give the illness its characteristic stamp. Further discussion of this issue can be found in the conclusion to this book. See also Introduction, n. 30.

63. The confusion of realms which can occur is suggested in remarks Schreber makes about what he refers to as "my *holy time*," a quasi-solipsistic period when he saw "fleeting-improvised-men," believed the whole of mankind to have perished, and "was filled with the most sublime ideas about God and the Order of the World" (M, 74, 80): "The impressions which rushed in upon me [then]," he writes, "were such a wonderful mixture of natural events and happenings of a supernatural nature that it is extremely difficult to distinguish mere dream visions from experiences in a waking state. . . . It is unavoidable therefore that my recollections of that time must in some measure bear the stamp of confusion" (M, 81).

64. Patients quoted in Bleuler, *Schizophrenic Disorders*, p. 490, and in Werner, *Comparative Psychology*, p. 418.

65. Bleuler, *The Schizophrenic Disorders*, p. 490.

66. See Thomas Szasz, "The Psychology of Bodily Feelings in Schizophrenia," *Psychosomatic Medicine* 19 (1957), 11–16, for a similar interpretation of self-mutilation. In other instances, however, self-injury seems to be an attempt to make things seem real. Renée, for example, would often feel an urge to hurt herself after things had begun to feel dreamlike; Sechehaye, *Autobiography of a Schizophrenic Girl*, p. 63.

67. The quotations are taken from Sidney Blatt, Jean G. Schimek, and C. Brooks Brenneis, "The Nature of the Psychotic Experience and Its Implications for the Therapeutic Process," in *The Psychotherapy of Schizophrenia*, ed. John S. Strauss, Malcolm Bowers, T. Wayne Downey, et al. (New York: Plenum, 1980), pp. 101–14, quotations from pp. 105–7. Blatt et al. refer to this as the "classic observation," accepted by Freud and, presumably, most later analysts. See Sigmund Freud, "Neurosis and Psychosis," and "The Loss of Reality in Neurosis and Psychosis," in *General Psychological Theory*, 185–89, 202–6; also *Civilization and Its Discontents*, trans. James Strachey (New York: Norton, 1962), p. 28. Franz Alexander says the schizophrenic "replaces his realistic perceptions with the wishful creation of his own fantasy, his delusions, illusions, and hallucinations"; "A Psychoanalyst Looks at Contemporary Art," in *Art and Psychoanalysis*, ed. William Philips (Cleveland: World, 1957), p. 358. Heinz Werner states that the "schizophrenic world of fantasy, like the child's play reality, has the value of the real, not because things appear true to nature, but rather because strong emotions bring them to life"; *Comparative Psychology of Mental Development*, p. 416.

68. Sartre, *Psychology of Imagination*, p. 189.

69. Bleuler, *The Schizophrenic Disorders*, p. 490.

70. Patient quoted in Meyer and Covi, "Experience of Depersonalization," p. 216. Positive moods in schizophrenia also tend to be devoid of normal, full-blooded forms of emotion. It has been pointed out that the elevated mood in schizophrenia is very different from the "infectious gaiety of true mania"; it seems to involve a kind of "exaltation" or "ecstasy" from which the observer feels alien. See Max Hamilton, ed., *Fish's Schizophrenia*, 2d ed. (Bristol: Wright, 1976), p. 53. I would argue that this "ecstasy" stems, at least in many cases, from a peculiarly solipsistic kind of experience that is quite alien to the normal human form of life. It involves feelings of constituting the world, not of being nurtured by it.

71. Quoted in Sechehaye, *A New Psychotherapy in Schizophrenia*, p. 147. See also M, 215, where Schreber says that "the continuation of all creation on our earth" rests entirely on himself (with his special relationship to God).

72. Quoted in ibid., pp. 147–48.

73. Schreber describes an oscillation between mood states which accompanies the quasi-solipsistic experience of "divine miracles." Though the oscillation is ascribed to God, one must recognize that it is in fact experienced by Schreber himself (as is explained in Chapter 2, in a sense Schreber *is* God): "Even for God Himself this situation is—as stated before—fraught with certain evils. His joy over newly created things can last only a short time and soon gives way to states of anxiety" (M, 196).

2. ENSLAVED SOVEREIGN, OBSERVED SPECTATOR

1. Karl Jaspers, *General Psychopathology*, trans. J. Hoenig and Marian Hamilton (Chicago: University of Chicago Press, 1963), p. 122.

2. In the *Blue Book*, Wittgenstein writes, "But mark, it is essential that everyone to whom I say this [that only what *I* see now is really seen] should be unable to understand me" (BBB, 65).

3. The above two passages in German: "Ich muss mich dabei auf Mitteilung der von mir empfangenen Eindrücke beschränken und kann hinsichtlich der Frage, um welche objektiven Vorgänge es sich bei jenen Veränderungen gehandelt hat, höchstens Vermutungen wagen. . . . Ercheinung *kleinere* Sonne" (M, orig. 135). "Ich bin mir wohl bewusst, wie phantastisch alles Derartige für andere Menschen klingen muss; ich gehe demnach auch nicht soweit zu behaupten, dass alles darüber Erzählte objektive Wirklichkeit gewesen ist; ich referiere nur, welche Eindrücke als Erinnerungen noch in meinem Gedächtnisse haften" (M, orig, 73).

4. Wittgenstein: "And therefore, if I utter the sentence 'Only I really see', . . . What, however, is wrong, is to think that I can *justify* this choice of notation" (BBB, 66). Statements from two other schizophrenic-type patients suggest a similar sense of separation from the objective or shared world: "Everything is reality now, but an outsider can never be shown this—it can only be believed." "All that I am experiencing is only mental, but if one has only an atom of faith one can understand the most impossible things"; quoted in Heinz Werner, *Comparative Psychology of Mental Development* (New York: International Universities Press, 1957), p. 417.

5. For a clear example of this oscillation between a private and a public domain, see Renée's description of her fear that the world is about to be destroyed; Marguerite Sechehaye, ed., *Autobiography of a Schizophrenic Girl* (New York: New American Library, 1970), p. 27.

6. As stated in the Introduction, I acknowledge that some schizophrenic delusions probably do fit the poor reality-testing formula. Thus I would not claim that all seeming deviations from the solipsistic mode must be manifestations of solipsism's inherent contradictions. However, many of these

instances of poor reality testing may involve delusions inspired by the perceptual peculiarities of the uncanny particularity experience (described in Chapter 3); this would mean they do share something with quasi-solipsism: a dependence on an attitude of isolation, withdrawal, and hyperconcentration.

7. "dass alles, was geschieht, auf mich bezogen wird" (M, orig, 262).

8. "für keineswegs ausgeschlossen möchte ich es aber halten, dass das damit verbundene Sehvermögen . . . ausschliesslich nach meiner Person gegebenen Richtung eben auf dasjenige, was mit mir und in meiner unmittelbaren Nähe geschieht sich beschränkt" (M, orig, 322). "die sogenannte 'Menschenspielerei' (die wundermässige Einwirkung) sich auf mich und *meine jeweilige nächste Umgebung* beschränkt" (M, orig, IV–V).

9. "in entsprechender Weise wiederholt einzelne spielende Mücken vor meinem Gesicht gewundert und auch diesmal *nur* in meiner unmittelbaren Nähe" (M, orig, 324).

10. One might be tempted to argue that (unlike Schreber) an autistic solipsist is writing only for himself, that is, not intending to communicate but only to express. Even in such a case, however, Wittgenstein might argue that, since language is inherently a social phenomenon (see his famous refutation of the very idea of a private language), using language at all necessarily involves at least some acceptance of the existence of others.

11. P. M. S. Hacker, *Insight and Illusion: Wittgenstein on Philosophy and the Metaphysics of Experience* (London: Oxford University Press, 1972), p. 186.

12. The original for a key sentence in the first passage has already been given (n. 8). For parts of the second passage, the original reads as follows: "Nachdem Gott zu mir in ausschliesslichen Nervenanhang getreten ist, bin ich für Gott in gewissem Sinn der Mensch schlechthin oder der einzige Mensch geworden, um den sich alles dreht, auf den alles, was geschieht, bezogen werden müsse und der also auch von seinem Standpunkte alle Dinge auf sich selbst beziehen solle. . . . Wenn ich z. B. ein Buch oder eine Zeitung lese, so meint man, dass die darin enthaltenen Gedanken meine eigenen Gedanken seien" (M, orig, 262–63).

13. See this chapter, "On Contradiction" section, for a similar instance: "My superiority . . . to be understood in *the most relative sense*" (M, 155).

14. "Hoffen doch, dass die Wollust einen Grad erreicht" (M, orig, 329).

15. Jonathan Lang, the patient quoted in Chapter 1, often speaks in this manner. Maria Lorenz has remarked on this tendency; see "Expressive Behavior and Language Patterns," *Psychiatry* 18 (1955), 362. Sheldon Bach describes it as part of a "narcissistic state of consciousness"; see "On the

Narcissistic State of Consciousness," *International Journal of Psychoanalysis* 58 (1977), 220.

16. "'Schmetterling—fand Aufnahme,' d. h. man hat es für möglich gehalten, dass ich nicht mehr wisse, was ein Schmetterling sei" (M, orig, 246).

17. Jaspers, *General Psychopathology*, p. 122.

18. Herbert A. Rosenfeld, "Analysis of a Schizophrenic State with Depersonalization," in Rosenfeld, *Psychotic States: A Psychoanalytical Approach* (London: Maresfield Reprints, 1965, 1982), pp. 13–33.

19. Antonin Artaud, *Antonin Artaud: Selected Writings*, ed. Susan Sontag (New York: Farrar, Straus and Giroux, 1976), p. 362.

20. A similar paradox is contained in other variants of what has been called the "influencing-machine delusion," a classic symptom of schizophrenia. See, for example, the case of Natalija presented by Victor Tausk in "On the Origin of the 'Influencing Machine' in Schizophrenia," which is discussed in Louis A. Sass, *Madness and Modernism* (New York: Basic Books, 1992), pp. 331–33.

21. This set of contradictions is also described in Sass, *Madness and Modernism*, pp. 324–27.

22. Arthur Schopenhauer, *The World as Will and Representation*, trans. E. F. J. Payne (New York: Dover, 1966), vol. 1, p. 332.

23. See discussion in Hacker, *Insight and Illusion*, p. 204; also p. 59, where Hacker points out the parallels with Hume's argument on "the nonencounterability of the self in experience."

24. Schopenhauer, *World as Will and Representation*, vol. 2, p. 491. In his early work, the *Tractatus Logico-Philosophicus*, Wittgenstein compares the relationship of the subject and his world to that of the eye and its field of sight, pointing out that "really you do *not* see the eye" (TLP, §5.633). In his later writings, Wittgenstein continued to use the metaphor of the eye and its visual field; see, e.g., BBB, 72.

25. My discussion here and at a number of points in the following several pages is indebted to the treatment of Wittgenstein's critique of solipsism offered by P. M. S. Hacker in *Insight and Illusion* (see, e.g., pp. 64, 189, 213 of his book).

26. Patients quoted in James Chapman, "The Early Symptoms of Schizophrenia," *British Journal of Psychiatry* 112 (1966), 232, and in R. D. Laing, *The Divided Self* (Harmondsworth: Penguin, 1965), p. 151.

27. I am, of course, speaking of the phenomenology of solipsism: solipsistic experience seems to demand the felt presence of an other consciousness who, in a sense (and paradoxically), seems to constitute the solipsist.

28. See Georg Henrik von Wright, "Biographical Sketch," in Norman Malcolm, *Ludwig Wittgenstein: A Memoir* (London: Oxford University

Press, 1958), p. 5. "The world is my idea" (or "my representation") is the first line of Schopenhauer's *World as Will and Representation* (p. 3). Schopenhauer states that Berkeley was the first to enunciate this insight, but he finds its sources in Descartes's skeptical reflections, which would make the insight coincident with the rise of modern philosophy.

It should be noted as well that, in all likelihood, Schopenhauer also influenced Wittgenstein's reaction *against* solipsism and idealism. Consider, in this connection, Schopenhauer's critique of Fichte and also his proto-Wittgensteinian statements, for example, that "a man becomes a philosopher by reason of a certain perplexity, from which he seeks to free himself," and that "theoretical egoism" (solipsism) can be found only in a madhouse and needs not so much a refutation as a cure. See *World as Will and Representation*, vol. 1, pp. 32, 104; also the Modern Library edition, *The Philosophy of Schopenhauer*, ed. Irwin Edman (New York: Modern Library, 1928), pp. 29, 66 (I have used the latter translation). On Schopenhauer's influence on Wittgenstein, see Patrick Gardiner, *Schopenhauer* (Baltimore: Penguin, 1963), pp. 85, 275–82.

29. On the later Wittgenstein as reacting against positions, especially solipsism and idealism, which had tempted him as a young man, see Hacker, *Insight and Illusion*, esp. pp. 59, 69, 75, 82. In a personal memoir of Wittgenstein, the philosopher J. N. Findlay argues that, even during his later period, Wittgenstein remained strongly attracted to solipsism, both in life and in thought; J. N. Findlay, "My Encounters with Wittgenstein," *Philosophical Forum* 4 (1972–73), 167–85. In my view, however, Findlay's interesting but rather mean-spirited article fails to recognize the importance, both personal and philosophical, of Wittgenstein's profound reaction *against* solipsism. Bryan Magee, who is sharply critical of Hacker's treatment of Wittgenstein and solipsism, takes the dissenting view that neither Schopenhauer nor Wittgenstein was ever a solipsist; *The Philosophy of Schopenhauer* (New York: Oxford University Press, 1985), pp. 286–315. As a point about explicit philosophical doctrines the issue is debatable; but if one understands solipsism more as a form of life or a kind of existential temptation, which in my view was what most concerned Wittgenstein, Magee seems to be missing the point. Also, given this focus, Hacker's emphasis on Wittgenstein's concern with similarities rather than differences among solipsism, idealism, and phenomenalism seems appropriate; *Insight and Illusion*, pp. 186, 216.

30. Iris Murdoch, *The Sovereignty of Good* (London: Routledge and Kegan Paul, 1970), p. 72.

31. See Ronald Clark, *The Life of Bertrand Russell* (London: Jonathan Cape, 1975), pp. 192, 204, 217.

32. I am taking some liberties with the say-versus-show distinction here.

33. "und daher auch jetzt noch, je nachdem neuere Eindrücke bald die eine, bald die andere Auffassung zu begünstigen scheinen, hin und herschwanke" (M, orig, 264n).

34. "sich in das Gefühl der Abhängigkeit von einem einzelnen Menschen, auf den man sonst in dem stolzen Bewusstsein einer unnahbaren Macht herabgesehen haben würde, hineinfinden" (M, orig, 164).

35. "Aller Unsinn (d. h. der Unsinn des Gedankenlesens und Gedankenfälschens) hebt sich auf. . . . Vergessen Sie nicht, dass alle Darstellung ein Unsinn ist. . . . Vergessen Sie nicht, dass das Weltende ein Widerspruch in sich selber ist" (M, orig, 182–83).

36. The main sources for this conception of the primary process are the famous chapters 6 and 7 of Freud's *The Interpretation of Dreams* (1900), Standard Edition, vols. 4 and 5.

37. For an example of such an interpretation of psychosis, see Charles Donnelly, "The Observing Self and the Development of Cohesiveness," *British Journal of Medical Psychology* 52 (1979), 277–79.

38. I have discussed these parallels in considerable detail in *Madness and Modernism*. Here I mention them briefly, mostly as a way of bringing out their relevance for an explication of certain contradictions of schizophrenic existence.

39. Michel Foucault, *The Order of Things: An Archaeology of the Human Sciences* (New York: Vintage, 1973), pp. 341, 364, 343.

40. Schopenhauer, *The World as Will and Representation*, vol. 1, pp. 5, 28, 30, 204, 332.

41. Hegel quoted in C. L. Griswold, Jr., "Plato's Metaphilosophy: Why Plato Wrote Dialogues," *Platonic Readings* (New York: Routledge and Kegan Paul, 1988), p. 150.

42. I explore Wittgenstein's criticism of tendencies to reduce consciousness or experience to something thinglike further in Chapter 3.

43. Foucault, *Order of Things*, p. 336.

44. Ibid., pp. 315, 310.

45. This kinship brings up a fascinating issue that I will only touch on here since it lies outside the scope of this phenomenological and interpretive study: the question of how we might account for or explain this remarkable similarity between the schizophrenic and the modern condition.

It is possible that the affinity is largely fortuitous: schizophrenic individuals might suffer from an abnormality of brain functioning that leads to forms of experience—involving alienation, hyper-self-consciousness, and fragmentation—which just happen to mimic aspects of the modern psyche (several recent neurobiological theories are consistent with this view; see the appendix to Sass, *Madness and Modernism*). It seems likely, however, that the modern social or cultural order would be significant, if not in creating, then at least in shaping some of the central symptoms of schizophrenia (perhaps by channeling the effects of more general neurophysiological abnormalities in a particular symptomatic direction). Whether one speaks of creating or only of shaping depends in large part on the mostly theoretical question of how one chooses to define schizophrenia—on whether, for instance, such signs and symptoms as autistic withdrawal, chronicity, and, perhaps, certain first-rank symptoms are treated as defining criteria of the illness or merely as commonly associated features. Various aspects of modernity might contribute to the development of the kinds of symptoms Schreber displays, whether by presenting particular difficulties or sources of anxiety for vulnerable individuals or by encouraging the development of certain kinds of symptomatic response (involving withdrawal, self-consciousness, and self-distancing). These would include the modern emphases on personal initiative, self-reliance, and individual responsibility; on individuality and inwardness; on self-contemplation and affective disengagement; on rationalism, relativism, and the capacity for reflection and mental abstraction; and on impersonality in many social relationships (for further discussion, see the epilogue to *Madness and Modernism*).

Daniel Paul Schreber is a particularly interesting case to consider from this latter viewpoint, because of the rather distinctive nature of the upbringing to which he seems likely to have been subjected by his father, an influential pedagogue whose theories of child rearing were fairly well known in the German-speaking world of the time. Elsewhere I have argued that these child-rearing techniques embody what Foucault describes in one of his books, *Discipline and Punish*, as the essential elements of the modern social order, the order of what he calls power\knowledge, namely, the disciplinary principle of "panopticism," and that these same (panoptical) elements permeate Schreber's own delusional system and general form of life (see Sass, "Schreber's Panopticism: Psychosis and the Modern Soul," *Social Research* 54 [1987], 101–47; Schreber's panoptical consciousness is also described in chapter 8 of *Madness and Modernism*). The term "panopticism" derives from the Panopticon, Jeremy Bentham's architectural design for buildings which would allow easy surveillance of subjugated populations, such as prison inmates, mental patients, or schoolchildren. The panoptical arrangement makes the individual feel constantly exposed to an external, normalizing gaze, thus subjecting him or her to the dictates of an authority that must ultimately be internalized; this arrangement encourages the development of a disciplinary kind of self-control which eradicates spontaneity, increases the sense of isolation and inwardness, and instills a relentlessly self-monitoring mode of consciousness.

Recent historical research suggests that Schreber's father was less fanatical and overtly sadistic, and his pedagogy less idiosyncratic, than has previously been assumed (see Zvi Lothane, *In Defense of Schreber: Soul Murder and Psychiatry* [Hillsdale, N.J.: Analytic Press, 1992], pp. 106–98). If this is true, it implies that Schreber's upbringing may not have been all that unusual given his cultural milieu; it suggests that the etiology of Schreber's illness might be, if not exactly typical, then at least exemplary of how schizophrenic symptoms can develop within the (panoptical) modern social order.

It is interesting that Schreber should manifest, in such clear form, both of the key features that Foucault describes in his two major works on the modern age (*Order of Things* and *Discipline and Punish*). Schreber's panopticism does seem to derive, in large part, from the social and familial context in which he existed and was reared. Whether one could say the same concerning his embodying of the doublet of modern thought is more debatable, though here one might point to the peculiar inwardness of the father's pedagogy, which emphasized controlling not just the behavior but also the experience of the child. Perhaps Schreber's early sense of having his thoughts and feelings under constant scrutiny contributed to his later tendency to focus on and objectify his own inner experiences, and also, possibly, to his sense of their profound, even constituting importance.

3. A VAST MUSEUM OF STRANGENESS

1. Quoted in Karl Jaspers, *General Psychopathology*, trans. J. Hoenig and M. Hamilton (Chicago: University of Chicago Press, 1963), p. 296: "No state can support itself. If the world grows poor, they must come and fetch me; they have to have someone to support the world; the world must be represented or the world will disappear." In the original German: "Sie müssen einen Weltsteller haben. Ohne Weltvertretung geht die Welt kaputt."; see Karl Hilfiker, "Die schizophrene Ichauflösung im All," *Allgemeine Zeitschrift für Psychiatrie* 87 (1927), 439–69, quotation from 442. For a brief discussion of this quotation, see Louis Sass, *Madness and Modernism* (New York: Basic Books, 1992), pp. 519–20, n. 8.

2. Jaspers, *General Psychopathology*, p. 98.

3. R. D. Laing, *The Divided Self* (Harmondsworth: Penguin, 1965), p. 158.

4. David Hume, *A Treatise of Human Nature*, Book I, Part iv, Section 5, 2d ed., ed. L. A. Selby-Bigge (Oxford: Clarendon Press, 1978), p. 244.

5. See E. B. Titchener, *A Textbook of Psychology* (New York: Macmillan,

1910), pp. 519, 528, 546, 272-73. A useful summary of Titchener can be found in Edna Heidbreder, *Seven Psychologies* (Englewood Cliffs, N. J.: Prentice-Hall, 1933), pp. 113-51, quotation from Titchener ("hard introspective labor") on p. 129.

6. Titchener describes minds of several kinds: "In minds of the verbal type, the abstract idea of honesty or pride is then just the word 'honesty' or 'pride' as it appears in internal speech. In minds of the visual type, the verbal ideas are accompanied (or under certain circumstances replaced) by conventional pictures: [e.g.] the idea of pride by the image of a strutting, swelling figure" (*Textbook*, p. 528). Titchener also mentions a third kind, the introspector "of pronounced kinesthetic type," who might, for instance, find the symbol for *infinity* "in the tendency to prolong the word, this prolongation being accompanied by the distinct impression of projecting it from the mouth and then following this projected word by definite bodily movements" (p. 517). Each of these three forms of phantom concreteness (verbal, visual, kinesthetic) would seem to have its analogues in schizophrenic experience; each may be implicated in particular kinds of symptoms, most likely involving abnormalities of language, conceptual thinking, and motor behavior (catatonic-type symptoms), respectively.

7. Williams James, *The Principles of Psychology*, vol. 1 (New York: Holt, 1890), pp. 301, 304, 298. Actually, James's attitude toward this phenomenon is rather complex and perhaps not entirely consistent. In other parts of the *Principles*, he is critical of a similar kind of reification; see, for example, his treatment of the substantive versus transitive elements of experience in the chapter "The Stream of Thought" and also the reservations expressed on pp. 183–98 and 336–40. But with regard to the nature of the self, James does seem to commit the error Wittgenstein criticizes. For more extensive discussion of this kind of self-fragmentation, in schizophrenia and in modernism, see Sass, *Madness and Modernism*, chap. 7, or "Introspection, Schizophrenia, and the Fragmentation of Self," *Representations* 19 (1987), 1–34.

8. I should say a few words about the relationship among the processes of passivization, detached concentration, distancing, and substantialization. Are we to conceptualize these as separate entities in some kind of causal and temporal relationship with each other or as aspects of a single process having a more logical kind of relationship?

It is difficult to write in a way that does not suggest a relative independence of the processes, implying, for example, that one process tends to occur first and only then gives rise to another one (e.g., concentration leading to substantialization, or the reverse). I suspect I have sometimes given this impression in this book. In many instances, however, the phenomena may better be conceived not as separate events but as aspects of a single process that we are simply describing or seeing from different points of view. Thus, concentration may be the subject pole of an experiential event which, from the object pole standpoint, would be described as substantialization. Concentration may not cause or bring about substantialization (or vice versa), for this implies a merely contingent relationship when in fact the two phenomena may be logically interdependent.

In other instances, however, one of the phenomena may actually occur first, then, as it were, bringing the others in its train. A person who willfully decides to concentrate might, for example, bring on a certain substantialization of her mental objects. Or the very specificity and objectness of a sensation (qualities that could themselves be based on some physiological change) could cause one to adopt an attitude of detached concentration, toward, for example, the normally unconscious sensations of one's own body (and this in turn would be likely to heighten the substantialized quality of the sensations). Still other cases may lie midway between these two models, with the processes existing both as aspects and as entities in a way that is somewhat difficult to describe or to conceive. The latter would be the sort of conceptually ambiguous psychological phenomenon Wittgenstein sometimes discussed—one that seems to lie between two paradigms and should not be completely assimilated to either one (as was the case with seeing-as, which is neither/both an instance of seeing and of thinking).

9. I do not mean to imply that all the philosophical questions Wittgenstein wants to rule out of bounds become meaningful and appropriate in this schizophrenic context in which the phenomenology is so much closer to the philosophical picture of a Cartesian metaphysics. It is still senseless to ask, for example, whether I can have your experience. My point is only that the phenomenology of the schizophrenic's inner world is in certain respects analogous to those seductive pictures that have misled so many thinkers into adopting a Cartesian philosophy of mind.

10. Marguerite Sechehaye, ed., *Autobiography of a Schizophrenic Girl* (New York: New American Library, 1970), p. 42; also see pp. 27, 52, 64, 88-89.

11. See Eugen Bleuler, *Dementia Praecox or the Group of Schizophrenias*, trans. J. Zinkin (New York: International Universities Press, 1950), pp. 97, 104. Also see Laing, *Divided Self*, chap. 10.

12. The loss of the I-sense need not be primarily a consequence; it can also be a cause of phantom concreteness. Thus, in cases where the representing or picturing is felt to be carried out by an other, the picturing may take on more of the qualities of normal external reality rather than those of the merely imagined. Since it is not felt to be constituted by *my* self, the subjectivized reality may come to look or feel more actual and concrete. R. D.

Laing explains this in *The Divided Self*: "A 'thought' belonging to the 'other' self tends to have some of the quality of a perception since it is received by the experiencing self neither as a product of its imagination nor as belonging to it. That is, the *other self* is the basis of an hallucination. An hallucination is an as-if perception of a fragment of the disintegrated 'other' self by a remnant (self-focus) retaining residual I-sense" (p. 158).

13. "Ich erinnere mich noch mit einigem Humor des überaus drolligen Eindrucks, welchen es machte, wenn diese zuletzt völlig gedankenlos gewordene und nur noch auf Augeneindrücke beschränkte Seele, sobald ich irgendeinen Gegenstand in meiner Nähe suchte, gewissermassen mitsuchte, d. h. zu meinen Augen mit heraussah" (M, orig, 192).

14. "nicht um eine rein mechanisch wirkende Kraft, sondern um etwas den *psychologischen Triebfedern* ähnliches handelt: 'Anziehend' ist eben auch für Strahlen desjenige, was interessiert" (M, orig, 11n). For an elaborated interpretation of Schreber's delusional cosmos of nerves and rays as an allegory of his own mind, see Louis A. Sass, "Schreber's Panopticism: Psychosis and the Modern Soul," *Social Research* 54 (1987), 101–48, which appears, somewhat altered, as Chap. 8 of Sass, *Madness and Modernism*.

15. Titchener, *A Textbook of Psychology*, p. 516. Titchener's own, quite visually oriented mode of introspective experience is particularly reminiscent of Schreber's mind's eye world of representations. Compare, for instance, Schreber's description of the "fasces of the Roman Lictors" with Titchener's introspectionist account of his own experience on hearing the sentence "infinity broods over all things"—an experience dominated, Titchener says, by the image of "a blue-black, dense, arched sky, which palpitated, as if with immense wings, over a solid convex surface—evidently the surface of the globe. *Infinity* was thus given as the spatial extent of the sky; broods as the wing-like movement" (*Textbook*, pp. 517–18).

Obviously, the introverted, self-scrutinizing schizophrenic and the Titchenerian introspector are not identical in all respects. For one thing, the introspection of the scientific psychologist takes place within an institutionalized context and setting, whereas the schizophenic's introspection tends to be a way of life. Also, the schizophrenic's introspection may be rooted to some extent in neurobiological abnormalities and so be less willful than is the ideologically, and perhaps temperamentally, motivated introspectionism of Titchener. Still, Titchener's insistence on the greater and more foundational reality of the reified results of his hard introspective labor does resemble the self-deceptions of a schizophrenic like Schreber, who believes he has discovered not simply a different, but a deeper and more valid vision of the universe. (For discussion of possible neurobiological underpinnings of schizophrenia, see the appendix of Sass, *Madness and Mod-*

ernism. On volitional or intentional factors in schizophrenia, see index entries under "act-affliction issue" in *Madness and Modernism*).

16. Though this more foundational mind's eye is not directly perceived, it is experienced in some implicit fashion in the quasi-solipsist's world—in the sense that it frames all the contents of experience as being "merely" subjective or representational. It does not exist as an objectified entity, as what Heidegger would call an ontic phenomenon. For discussion of similar aspects of schizophrenic delusion, but in a Heideggerian perspective, see Louis A. Sass, "Heidegger, Schizophrenia, and the Ontological Difference," *Philosophical Psychology* 5 (1992), 109–32.

17. See, for example, Kurt Goldstein, "Methodological Approach to the Study of Schizophrenic Thought Disorder," in *Language and Thought in Schizophrenia*, ed. J. S. Kasanin, (New York: Norton, 1964), pp. 17–40. See also Heinz Werner, *Comparative Psychology of Mental Development* (New York: International Universities Press, 1957), p. 371, where it is argued that the separate and thinglike existence of thoughts is a "concreteness" born of "regression from the higher level of the normal civilized man."

18. The use of metaphors derived from the physical world and sensory experience can hardly be taken to indicate either cognitive deficit or hyperreflexivity on the patient's part. As philosophers have often pointed out, a great many words referring to mental activity are explicit or faded metaphors based on physical action or sensory experience—for example, "grasping" an idea; on Locke's version of this point, see Hannah Arendt, *The Life of the Mind*, Vol. 1: *Thinking* (New York: Harcourt Brace Jovanovich, 1971), p. 31. Here I am arguing that schizophrenic-type distancing gives certain individuals an additional reason for adopting such modes of expression, especially those of a particularly reified and mechanistic sort.

19. Thus, whereas the Artaud passage quoted in Chapter 2 shows the cryptic abstractness of schizophrenia, this next passage perfectly illustrates phantom concreteness.

20. Antonin Artaud, *Antonin Artaud: Selected Writings*, ed. Susan Sontag (New York: Farrar, Straus, and Giroux, 1976), p. 60. For a more academic description of this kind of reflexive and empty consciousness, see one of Artaud's letters from 1932 (p. 293).

The "beak of a real dove" piercing the "confused mass of states" is an intriguing, if ambiguous, image. It might refer to an intruding awareness of the existence of an objective reality, a reality that does not need to be represented in order to exist. Could it be that a residual or implicit awareness of such a reality is what periodically shatters the subject's ability to believe in, and thus to continue constituting, the phenomenal reality that the subject does perceive (thus piercing the confused mass of [mental?] states)?

21. On the impossibility of representing representation, and the destructive consequences of attempting simultaneously to depict the same being as both subject and object, see Hubert Dreyfus and Paul Rabinow, *Michel Foucault: Beyond Structuralism and Hermeneutics* (Chicago: University of Chicago Press, 1982), pp. 25–27.

22. In my opinion, the world catastrophe experience (at least in many cases) is best understood as the culminating moment of a solipsistic process whereby the world is gradually derealized. In this I conflict with a view Freud proposed in his study of Schreber, one that has been adopted by most subsequent psychoanalysts who have addressed the question. According to Freud, the world catastrophe experience is something that occurs at the beginning of a psychotic episode, since it is the symbolic, psychological manifestation of the key development that initiates the psychotic process: namely, withdrawal of cathexes from the external world (this refers to withdrawal of libidinal attachment to, or investment in, the world). Supposedly, delusions and hallucinations occur later, for they are attempts at a re-cathexis of the world. Freud, however, admits that the usual sequence of symptoms is not consistent with his interpretation: he acknowledges that in Schreber's case and in many others the delusions of persecution actually precede "the phantasy of the end of the world"; see Sigmund Freud, "Psychoanalytic Notes upon an Autobiographical Account of a Case of Paranoia (Dementia Paranoides)," in *Three Case Histories*, ed. Philip Rieff (New York: Collier Books, 1963), p. 176. Freud accounts for this complication very tendentiously, implying that in such cases (which are, in fact, the majority) "the detachment of the libido from people—and things . . . happens silently [unconsciously, perhaps?]; we received no intelligence of it, but can only infer it from subsequent events" (p. 174). See Sass, *Madness and Modernism*, pp. 523–24, n. 46, for a bit more discussion of this issue.

23. Jaspers, *General Psychopathology*, pp. 98, 100, 106.

24. "dass es nicht mir zufällig zufliegende, sondern jeweilig um meinetwillen neuerschaffene Wesen sind" (M, orig, 242).

25. "Diese Tiere erscheinen bei ganz bestimmten Gelegenheiten und in ganz bestimmter Abwechslung fortwährend in meiner Nähe. . . . nicht als schon von früher her vorhandene, nur zufällig in meine Nähe getriebene, sondern als jeweilig neu erschaffene Wesen" (M, orig, 241).

26. See Sass, *Madness and Modernism*, chap. 2. See also J. H. Plokker, *Art from the Mentally Disturbed*, trans. I. Finlay (Boston: Little, Brown, 1964), p. 56.

27. On delusional percept, see Kurt Schneider, *Clinical Psychopathology* (New York: Grune and Stratton, 1959), pp. 104–15; Jaspers, *General Psychopathology*, pp. 99–103; Karl Koehler, "Delusional Perception and Delu-

sional Notion Linked to a Perception," *Psychiatria Clinica*, 9 (1976), 45–58; C. S. Mellor, "Delusional Perception," *British Journal of Psychiatry*, 159 supp. 14 (1991), 104–7.

28. Examples from Max Hamilton, ed., *Fish's Schizophrenia*, 2d ed. (Bristol: John Wright and Sons, 1976), p. 41 (an example taken from Schneider); and Mellor, "Delusional Perception," p. 105.

29. But see the discussion of the work of the German psychiatrists Paul Matussek and Klaus Conrad, in Hamilton, *Fish's Schizophrenia*, pp. 40–44, 157–62. See also Paul Matussek, "Studies in Delusional Perception," in *The Clinical Roots of the Schizophrenia Concept*, ed. John Cutting and Michael Shepherd (Cambridge: Cambridge University Press, 1987), pp. 89–103.

30. This phrase is from Maurice Merleau-Ponty, *The Phenomenology of Perception*, trans. Colin Smith (London: Routledge and Kegan Paul, 1962), p. 63.

31. This experience is reminiscent of, but also distinguishable from, certain kinds of aesthetic epiphanies. See note 43 in this chapter. Incidentally, one passage from Wittgenstein's notes suggests not only that he was prone to something like the mute particularity experience but that he recognized its possible affinity to the experience of the insane: "During a dream and even *long* after we have woken up, words occurring in the dream can strike us as having the greatest significance. Can't we be subject to the same illusion when awake? I have the impression that *I* am sometimes liable to this nowadays. The insane often seem to be like this" (CV, 65).

32. M. O'C. Drury, "Conversations with Wittgenstein," in *Recollections of Wittgenstein*, ed. Rush Rhees, 2d ed. (Oxford: Oxford University Press, 1984), p. 219.

33. Bleuler, *Dementia Praecox*, pp. 141, 125.

34. Marguerite Sechehaye, *A New Psychotherapy in Schizophrenia* (New York: Grune and Stratton, 1956), p. 147.

35. Robert Musil, *Five Women*, trans. Eithne Wilkins and Ernst Kaiser (New York: Dell, 1965), p. 127.

36. See Eugene Minkowski, "Findings in a Case of Schizophrenic Depression," in *Existence*, ed. Rollo May (New York: Simon and Schuster, 1958), p. 136. Also see Manfred Bleuler's discussion of the fact that schizophrenics who were previously inaccessible may suddenly begin acting in a normal and competent manner, sometimes when circumstances have forced them out of their old patterns and into new forms of practical activity; *The Schizophrenic Disorders*, trans. Siegfried M. Clemens (New Haven: Yale University Press, 1978), pp. 480–81.

37. Sechehaye, *Autobiography of a Schizophrenic Girl*, pp. 123, 118. Silvano Arieti, *The Interpretation of Schizophrenia*, 2d ed. (New York: Basic, 1974), pp. 120–21.

38. Sigmund Freud, "The Uncanny," in *Studies in Parapsychology*, ed. Philip Rieff (New York: Collier Books, 1963), pp. 19–62, quotations from pp. 20, 41. Freud, however, is not explicitly concerned with schizoid or schizophrenic-type experiences per se.

39. Marcel Jean, ed., *The Autobiography of Surrealism* (New York: Viking, 1980), p. 6 (translation slightly altered). In his diaries, Giorgio de Chirico wrote at length about the mood state he was attempting to capture in his famous paintings, and what he recounts is strikingly similar to the experience of mute particularity described by Wittgenstein and Schreber. For de Chirico too the experience was associated with a certain passive hyperawareness (exacerbated in his case by feeling physically ill at the time he had the vision in question). Such a mode of experience came to be sought by many of the surrealists, both as a source of aesthetic inspiration and even as a preferred mode of life; see Sass, *Madness and Modernism*, chap. 2.

40. Erich Kahler, *The Tower and the Abyss: An Inquiry into the Transformation of Man* (New York: Viking, 1957), pp. 90, 159, 138, 170.

41. André Breton, *Nadja* (New York: Grove Press, 1960), pp. 19-20. Incidentally, the passivization of the schizophrenic patient experiencing mute particularity, or of Wittgenstein's "philosopher," need not involve a literal, physical inactivity, though it often does.

42. Diane Arbus, *Diane Arbus* (Millerton, N.Y.: Aperture Monographs, with the Museum of Modern Art, 1972), p. 1.

43. Arbus's journal entries, which serve as an introduction to the main collection of her photographs, provide excellent descriptions of this mood state; see ibid., pp. 1–15.

I am not claiming that all experiences to which the terms "mute" or "intransitive particularity" might conceivably be applied are of the alienated, hyperreflexive, and perhaps pathological sort discussed here. In romantic and symbolist notions of the symbol, much emphasis was also placed on a kind of intransitivity, that is, on the immanence or self-containment of the aesthetic value and meaning of the object perceived in a moment of aesthetic epiphany. James Joyce speaks, for example, of the aesthetic image which is apprehended as "one thing," "self-bounded and self-contained upon the immeasurable background of space or time which is not it," apprehended in its *quidditas* by a mind arrested in a "luminous silent stasis of esthetic pleasure"; *A Portrait of the Artist as a Young Man* (New York: Viking, 1965), pp. 212–13. Like mute particularity in Wittgenstein, Schreber, and Arbus, this postromantic mode of vision also requires being cut off from action and from life—a state of passivization, isolation, and detached contemplation (see Frank Kermode, *Romantic Image* [London: Fontana, 1971], pp. 13, 18).

But there are also important differences between mute particularity and the symbolist epiphany. In the epiphany, the experience of the object's *quidditas* does not seem to imply some hidden but potentially specifiable meaning or some other, more real version of the object lying elsewhere. The experience is thus more purely and simply intransitive in nature; it is not imbued with the kind of doubledness or pseudo-*trans*itivity which, in the mute particularity experience, makes the visible object seem a cipher to be decoded or a pale copy of itself. Consequently, the epiphany is more a condition of grace—without that tantalizing doubledness, that ever-frustrating feeling that reality is always at a remove. One might say that, whereas the mute particularity experience seems to be transitive but really is not, the epiphany both seems and is truly *intransitive*. Another way of putting the difference is to say that in one case essence and existence are sundered whereas in the other they are not. Unlike mute particularity, the epiphany involves a sense neither of free-floating meaning nor of the brute substantiality of things but, instead, a plenitude of being in which pleasure can simultaneously be taken in both the whatness and the thereness of the world.

The intransitive particularity of schizoid experience has more in common with a central aspect of the *post*modernist sensibility—namely, what has been described as a certain preference for allegory over symbol or, more accurately put, for a mode of perception or expression in which everything is seen (or presented) as being but a copy or a representation of something that lies elsewhere. Actually, since this something can never be found—it does not exist—we could characterize the postmodernist mood or sensibility as pseudo-allegorical; and this is akin to the pseudo-transitivity of the mute particularity experience. For discussion of these aesthetic modes, see Louis A. Sass, "Psychoanalysis, Romanticism, and the Nature of Aesthetic Consciousness—with Reflections on Modernism and Postmodernism," to appear in *Development and the Arts: Critical Perspectives*, ed. Margery Franklin and Bernard Kaplan (Hillsdale, N.J.: Erlbaum, in press).

44. W. Ronald D. Fairbairn, *An Object-Relations Theory of the Personality* (New York: Basic, 1954), pp. 20–21.

45. Sechehaye, *Autobiography of a Schizophrenic Girl*, p. 33. Renée's Land of Enlightenment/Madness is also the "Land of Commandment," for there she loses a sense of her volitional capacity (p. 43).

CONCLUSION

1. But see Chapter 2, n. 45 for some discussion of the question of origins.

2. Harold Searles, "Sexual Processes in Schizophrenia," in *Collected Papers on Schizophrenia and Related Subjects* (New York: International Universities Press, 1965), pp. 429–42, see especially pp. 431–33. Robert

White, "The Mother-Conflict in Schreber's Psychosis," *International Journal of Psychoanalysis* 42 (1961), 55–73.

3. Elias Canetti, *Crowds and Power*, trans. Carol Stewart (New York: Continuum, 1973), 434–62.

4. Morton Schatzman, *Soul Murder: Persecution in the Family* (New York: New American Library, 1973). William Niederland, *The Schreber Case: Psychoanalytic Profile of a Paranoid Personality* (Hillsdale, N.J.: The Analytic Press/Erlbaum, 1984). The positions of Schatzman and Niederland are not identical, but both emphasize the power relations inherent in the patient's upbringing. Zvi Lothane offers an important critique of these and other writers on Schreber in *In Defense of Schreber: Soul Murder and Psychiatry* (Hillsdale, N.J.: Analytic Press, 1992).

5. I am concerned in this book with the nature of Schreber's mode of experience in adulthood, not with childhood origins or precursors. But this is not to say I would deny the importance of the life-historical events of the kind discussed by Niederland and by Schatzman; I accept, for example, that the "one" or "God" to whom Schreber refers is associated with his father, who continues to live in Schreber's consciousness as a sort of disguised epistemological introject. It should be noted, however, that Schatzman and Niederland do not pursue very extensively, if at all, the phenomenological structure of the son's lived-world, preferring to focus on issues pertaining to the content of the delusions. For this reason, perhaps, they fail to note the peculiarly epistemological way in which the theme of power is experienced by Schreber. On the role of Schreber's upbringing, see n. 45 of Chapter 2.

6. Canetti, *Crowds and Power*, p. 441.

7. In her memoir of schizophrenic illness, *Operators and Things* (Cambridge, Mass.: Arlington, 1958), Barbara O'Brien describes a vision of a world divided into two such forms of being. The words below, spoken by Burt, an inner voice who is himself an "operator," describes a power relationship that is essentially epistemological, manifested in "knowing":

> "Yes," Burt said. "Operators move about in the flesh. So far as surface appearance is concerned, Operators are identical with Things. No Thing would be able to distinguish one from the other, the Operators can distinguish them easily. An Operator need only extend and contact the individual's mind and he knows instantly whether he's tuned in on an Operator or a Thing."
>
> I scrutinized their soft, grey, fuzzy shapes. "Sure, we have bodies," Nicky said. "What you're looking at now are pictures of ourselves that we're projecting."

And where were the bodies?

"Close by," Nicky grinned. "Don't come looking for us, though. We'd blank you out before you could reach us." . . .

Burt cleared his throat. "The one great difference between an Operator and a Thing is the construction and ability of the mind. Operators are born with special brain cells known as the battlement. With these cells, an Operator can extend and probe into the mind of a Thing. He can tap the Thing's mind and discover what is going on there, and even feed thoughts to the Thing's mind in order to motivate it. The mental difference is one of ability, not one of quality. Operators, like Things, may be stupid or intelligent. But that one difference permits the Operators to rule the Things." (P. 35)

8. John Berger, *Ways of Seeing* (London: BBC and Penguin, 1972), p. 47.

9. Karl Jaspers, *General Psychopathology*, trans. J. Hoenig and M. W. Hamilton (Chicago: University of Chicago Press, 1963), p. 98.

10. See K. T. Fann, *Wittgenstein's Conception of Philosophy* (Berkeley: University of California Press, 1969), p. 87.

11. Schreber: "Can there be any prospect more terrible for a human being so highly gifted in such various ways, as I may say of myself without conceit, than the prospect of losing one's reason and perishing an imbecile?" (M, 212). "Every time my thinking activity ceases God instantly regards my mental powers as extinct . . . ('the dementia')" (M, 166).

12. As Schreber describes it, the relationship between watching rays and watched nerves seems to require a certain degree of distance. Too little distance between the two means a collapsing of the difference on which the being of each depends; too much distance implies mutual unawareness or indifference. Hence the advent of reflexive self-consciousness is sometimes implied by the rays pulling away from Schreber or from the nerves—as in this passage from the *Memoirs*, p. 201—but at other times by the approaching of the rays—as in a passage I quoted a few pages earlier (M, 206).

13. Other methods Schreber used to overcome "compulsive thinking" included playing the piano, counting to himself, repeating nonsense syllables, and losing himself in what he called the "bellowing miracle" (M, 143–44, 233, 176, 227). As a way of drowning out the voices and dissolving the concentration of self-consciousness, he would sometimes begin shouting and yelling. Such behavior is usually interpreted as a sign of a loss of the capacity for self-control, perhaps as a consequence of regression to an infantile state; see, for example, I. Hermann, "Some Aspects of Psychotic Regression, a Schreber Study," *International Review of Psychoanalysis* 7 (1980).

Ironically, however, Schreber's bellowing was actually motivated by a desire to escape a condition of exacerbated self-awareness and self-control (as he himself explains; see M, 227–28). And Schreber was quite aware that this kind of behavior looked wild and nonsensical to others. Of the effect of the "bellowing miracle," headaches, and other sufferings, he wrote, "This rapid change in my condition gives the overall impression of madness and my whole life therefore carries this stamp, the more so as my surroundings are made up mostly of madmen who themselves add to all sorts of mad things happening" (M, 202).

14. "Für mich is nun subjectiv gewiss, dass mein Körper . . ." (M, orig, 277).

15. It is not uncommon for schizophrenic patients to become preoccupied with staring at themselves in the mirror, especially in the early phases of the illness. In French psychiatry this is known as the "signe du miroir"; see Paul Abély, "Le signe du miroir dans les psychoses et plus spécialement dans la démence précoce," *Annales Médico-Psychologiques* (1930), 28–36.

16. The intimate connection between femininity, bodily experience, and the condition of being an object of consciousness is shown in the following passage: "'Is he not unmanned yet?' God's rays frequently mocked me about a supposedly imminent unmanning as 'Miss Schreber'; an expression used frequently and repeated *ad nauseam* was: 'You are to be *represented* as given to voluptuous excesses'" (M, 119–20).

Schreber describes the experience of feminization, whether from direct sensual pleasure or from the mirror experience, as involving "Blessedness"—a state expressed, he says, by a line from Schiller's "Ode to Joy": "Voluptuousness is given even to the worm [especially to the worm, would perhaps be more accurate], but it's the Cherub who stands before God" (M, 208).

17. "Oder ich habe, um mich eines Oxymorons zu bedienen, in dem von Gott wider mich geführten Kampfe Gott selbst auf meiner Seite gehabt, d. h. bin in der Lage gewesen, seine eigenen Eigenschaften und Kräfte als eine unbedingt wirksame Schutzwaffe zu meiner Selbstverteidigung in das Feld zu fuhren" (M, orig, 61n).

18. Freud quoted in Victor Tausk, "On the Origin of the 'Influencing Machine' in Schizophrenia" (1919), *Psychoanalytic Quarterly* 2 (1933), 542. Also see Sigmund Freud, "Psychoanalytic Notes upon an Autobiographical Account of a Case of Paranoia (Dementia Paranoides)," in *Three Case Histories*, ed. Philip Rieff (New York: Collier Books, 1963), p. 181.

INDEX

Library of Congress Cataloging-in-Publication Data

Sass, Louis Arnorsson.
The paradoxes of delusion : Wittgenstein, Schreber, and the schizophrenic mind / Louis A. Sass.
p. cm.
Includes bibliographical references and index.
ISBN 0-8014-2210-8
1. Schizophrenia. 2. Wittgenstein, Ludwig, 1889–1951. 3. Schreber, Daniel Paul, 1842–1911. 4. Psychiatry—Philosophy. 5. Delusions. I. Title.
RC514.S3163 1993
616.89'001—dc20 93-24931